martin Sorell

AN ANTHOLOGY OF
TWENTIETH CENTURY
FRENCH POETRY

AN
ANTHOLOGY OF
TWENTIETH CENTURY
FRENCH POETRY

COMPILED AND
TRANSLATED BY
WILLIAM ALWYN

1969
CHATTO & WINDUS
LONDON

Published by
Chatto and Windus Ltd
42 William IV Street
London W.C.2

*

Clarke, Irwin and Co Ltd
Toronto

Printed in Great Britain by
R. and R. Clark Ltd
Edinburgh

To the Memory

of

ROBERT DESNOS

Robert, within this book your friends walk by your side
Some living still and some like you have died
Your words alone speak of the deathless bond
That binds you to them from that most cruel land
Which penned you in but could not clamp your mind

Some think that poets are not men
Built to sustain the strain of physical endurance —
They need but think of you
Your poor bones wracked by famine and by fever
Yet for us for ever
You gathered beauty till the end

Acknowledgements

The following acknowledgements are due to the publishers and copyright owners for permission to translate the poems contained in this anthology.

To Gallimard (Éditions de la NRF) for the poems by Guillaume Apollinaire, Louis Aragon, Joë Bousquet, André Breton, Blaise Cendars, René Char, Robert Desnos, Paul Eluard, Léon-Paul Fargue, André Frénaud, Eugène Guillevic, Max Jacob, Valery Larbaud, Patrice de La Tour de Pin, Henri Michaux, Jacques Prévert, Raymond Queneau, Saint-John Perse and Jules Supervielle.

To Éditions du Mercure de France for the poems by Yves Bonnefoy, Paul Claudel, Francis Jammes, Pierre Jean Jouve, Paul Reverdy and Saint-Pol-Roux.

To Éditions Pierre Seghers for the poems by René Cadou and Marie-Jeanne Durry.

To Éditions de Minuit for the poems by Robert Pinget and Nathalie Sarraute.

To Éditions Stock for the poems by Marie Noël.

To Nouvelles Éditions Meridian for the poems by Leo Ferré.

To Messrs Routledge for the poem by Paul Valéry.

Personal acknowledgements are also due to M. Louis Aragon for his approval of the translations of his poems; to Madame Nathalie Sarraute for granting permission to translate three of her '*Tropismes*'; and to M. Leo Ferré for permission to include the lyrics of his songs.

Contents

viii

ix

x

xi

Epilogue

SAINT-POL-ROUX

Preface

AN anthology of contemporary writing in any language imposes many responsibilities on the compiler. A living art is in a continual state of flux; particularly is this true of the poetic art. New poets spring up like mushrooms and some as quickly disappear. In the case of younger poets there is little to guide the anthologist except his own taste and judgement. A reputation may be ephemeral, so he is wise if he ignores mere reputation and prefers to pin his faith in actual achievement, ignoring, when he can, contemporary critical opinion and trusting to his own experience. For this reason a contemporary anthology, if it is honest, is an adventure in personal taste–and this anthology is nothing if not personal.

The poems I have chosen are those which have given me especial pleasure, poems which have stimulated in me the desire to share my pleasure with others, and, through my translations, introduce the English reader to a vital and beautiful art. A book designed for pleasure requires no erudite introductory essay. If the reader's interest is roused by the poetry itself, then no doubt he will turn to other sources for detailed information.

But before the reader ventures into this new realm of French poetry I should perhaps make the following observations.

French literature, painting and music, have always been fertile grounds for experiment. Although the French creative artist is steeped in tradition and remains faithful to tradition, his native inventive wit leads him always in search of fresh modes of expression. And nowhere is this more evident than in poetry. Surrealism was born in France and among its apostles were André Breton, Aragon, Eluard, Desnos, and Queneau. Of these some remained iconoclasts but others, such as Eluard, Aragon and Desnos, combined surrealism with traditional, or semi-traditional, forms of versification. But, whether traditionalist or surrealist or both, each infused his poetry with beauty–and the exquisite sensitivity of the French poet to beauty gives it its own individual quality. Love of art is love of beauty, and in French poetry this seems an inexhaustible fountain.

Of the traditionalists Paul Valéry was the most distinguished. *Le cimetière marin* (1920), noble in formal design and unique in the intensity of its philosophic and poetic utterance, had as great an influence on French poetry as did Eliot's *The Waste Land* (1922) on English poets. A second influence, equally as potent in the younger poets, is the work of Saint-John Perse, whose fine rhetoric and inventive imagination owes little either to his contempories or to tradition, and who has created his own poetic world, a world which has some affinity to that of William Blake's Prophetic Books.

In 1940 France was invaded and occupied; no commentary, however brief, can neglect the importance of this catastrophe on the poets of France. They suffered the occupation with stoicism and wrote and fought for the resistance movement with supreme courage and selflessness. Some of them were killed, some died in concentration camps, but from resistance sprang some of their greatest poetry—poetry that was printed underground and circulated surreptitiously as an inspiration to their compatriots. A renaissance of French poetry took place in the *maquis* and its spirit is alive today.

Guillaume Apollinaire

(ROME 1880–PARIS 1918)

Poet, essayist, dramatist, apostle of the avant-garde (*Alcools*, 1913), and pioneer of typographical verse (*Calligrammes*, 1914). Apollinaire served with distinction in the first world war. Severely wounded in the head in 1916 he died two years later in the 'Spanish influenza' epidemic of 1918.

THE GIRL WITH RED HAIR

Behold in me a man of sensibility
Knowing life and death as well as mortal man can know
Experienced in the sorrows and the joys of love
Knowing how to propagate ideas
Knowing several languages
Having travelled here and there
Having seen the war in both Artillery and Infantry
Wounded in the head trepanned and chloroformed
Having lost the best of friends in this frightful strife
I know the old and new as well as any man can know them
And no longer worried by the war
Between ourselves my friends and just for us
In my opinion this long wrangle about tradition and innovation means
            Order or Adventure
You whose mouth is formed in the image of God's mouth
A mouth extremely orderly
Shew indulgence when you compare us
To those who once were order in perfection
Now seeking new adventure everywhere

We are not enemies
We want to give you vast and strange dominions
Where budding mystery waits for those to pluck it
New fires are there and colours yet unseen
A thousand unsuspected fantasies
Which must be made reality
We want to see that wide and gracious country where
                     all is quiet
There is a time for hunting and for turning back
Pity us who always battle at the frontiers
Of the future and infinity
Pity us our errors pity us our sins
See how Summer comes the violent season
And my youth is dead as dead as Springtime
O Sun this is the time of ardent Reason
               And I still wait
To follow her and see the sweet and noble shape
She takes for me to love alone
She draws me as iron by a magnet She comes
               Enchanting and adorable
               A girl with red hair
Her head is flecked with gold you might have said
An everlasting lightning flash
Or flames that flaunt
Among the fading roses

But laugh laugh at me
Men from everywhere but especially people here
There are so many things I dare not tell you
So many things you would not let me say
Have pity on me

A CLOUD OF DUST

A horseman rides in the valley
A young girl thinks of him
And the ships at Mytilene
And cold steel glinting

And how they plucked the burning rose
With eyes that blazed with fire
And felt the sun on smiling lips
Where kisses stray no more

FÊTE

Fire of fireworks forged in steel
How enchanting this display is
      Craftsman's artificial craft
Mixing courage with the graces

Two star-shells
Pink explosions
Rosy breasts exposed revealing
Nipples impudently posing
LOVE HE KNEW
      Proud epitaph

Poet hiding in the forest
Glances with a careless eye
      At his pistol's safety catch
And at matchless roses dying
Orient roses in the west
Suddenly his head relaxes
By a falling rose reminded
Of the soft curve of a thigh

3

Air replete with drunken terror
Filtered from the winking stars
Shells caress the perfumed breath
Of night where you repose at last
Roses mortified in death

Louis Aragon

(NEUILLY-SUR-SEINE 1897–   )

Poet, novelist and essayist, Aragon was in the forefront
of the surrealist movement (*Feu de Joie*, 1920; *Movement
Perpetuel*, 1925). He is married to the distinguished
novelist Elsa Triolet who has been the inspiration of
much of his best work (*Les Yeux d'Elsa*, 1942; *Le Fou
d'Elsa*, 1964). A dedicated communist, Aragon was
whole-heartedly involved in the Resistance during the
German occupation of France. *La Diane Française*, 1945,
includes many of the poems written during this period
for circulation underground. This collection is also
made notable by Aragon's revival of traditional verse
forms.

THE POETIC ART

For my friends who died in May
Though all time shall pass away

Let my rhymes contrive a spell
Blinding tears cannot dispel

And let every living thing
That changes with the changing wind

Sharpen in their deathless name
The pallid weapon of our shame

Married words words crucified
Rhymes instead of crimes decried

Coupled to a coupled thought a
Double sound of oars in water

Rhymes banal as falling rain
Shining on a window pane

Like a mirror masquerading
Blossoms at the bosom fading

Boy who bowls a hoop the gleam
Of moonlight on a placid stream

Lavender in linen cupboard
Childhood perfume half remembered

Rhymes rhymes in ceaseless flood
Surging with the heat of blood

Remind us ever and again
Of men's ferocity to men

When our feeble heart beats less
Waken from forgetfulness

Light again the lamps extinct
Let the empty glasses chink

My song alone will always stay
With my friends who died in May

THERE IS NO HAPPY LOVE

Nothing is acquired by man neither force
Nor frailty nor heart and when he thinks
To spread his wings his shadow forms a cross
And when he grasps at happiness it shrinks
His life is one of strange and sad divorce
        There is no happy love

His life resembles soldiers stripped of arms
Who have been chosen for another fate
What use their rising at the dawn's alarms
If night reveals them lost and desperate
Restrain your tears Life holds no further charms
There is no happy love

My dearest love my love my aching wound
I bear you in me like a stricken bird
And those who heedless watch us on our round
Repeat my woven phrases word by word
Then suddenly in your great eyes are drowned
There is no happy love

Time teaches us to live but not until
We cry too late by night in unison
Regrets are payment for the merest thrill
And pain demanded for a trivial song
The tuned guitar must sob or else be still
There is no happy love

There is no love that is not melancholy
There is no love for which we are not slain
No love but that which withers through our folly
And love of country is a dead refrain
There is no love that does not live on tears
There is no happy love
But it is ours

ELSA AT HER MIRROR
(1943)

This was at the nadir of our tragedy
A whole long day seated at her mirror
She combed her golden hair I thought I saw
Her patient hands calm the fire's intensity
This was at the nadir of our tragedy

A whole long day seated at her mirror
She combed her golden hair it seemed to me
This was at the nadir of our tragedy
A tune plucked from a harp subconsciously
A whole long day seated at her mirror

She combed her golden hair it seemed to me
Her memories she martyred in self-torture
Throughout a whole long day before her mirror
Fanning the flowering fire's immensity
No need for words she sat there silently

Her memories she martyred in self-torture
This was at the nadir of our tragedy
The world resembled that accursed mirror
With fire and comb her hair shone silkily
Lighting the corners of my memory

This was at the nadir of our tragedy
As sure as every week there comes a Thursday

Throughout a whole long day of memory
She saw afar off dying in her mirror

One by one the actors in our tragedy
Those in this world we least could spare

You know their names no need for words from me
Or what those flames at night-time signify

And when she rose at last so silently

Her golden hair was mirrored in the fire

8

FOR TOMORROW

You for whom this early spring makes
Magic punctuate my stanzas
Inspiration at the onset
Lost as sudden in a sunbeam
Now perpetuates in cadence

See the Seine in April sunshine
Dance like Cecily's first ballet
Or like golden pellets glancing
Under arch of stone or grating
Certain charm in town and valley

Quays as gay as carnaval
Bedazzled by the light of day
Light alights on splendid palace
Lighting here and there at random
I delight in my own way

Recklessly I play the truant
Owing nothing to Silenus
Drunk with colour lips and roses
Roses piled in florists' windows
Singing lips of girls in chorus

MAN ALONE

Man alone is a flight of stairs
Nothing leads anywhere
And all the doors of palaces
Are inhuman and destitute

Man alone has crooked arms
Streaky breath and eyes impaired
Nowhere to lay his head
He sleeps with a prostitute

Man alone has fingers of wind
Given to him to fan the ashes
No pleasure can he find
Save in the dust

Man alone has no face
He is but glass in the rain
And tears that rust and stain
Fall on the land

He is a letter gone astray
Bearing a wrong address
What hand could tear it
Said Tenderness

FUGUE

Joy comes in threes
A lyre strums the tune
Joy hums in trees
How I cannot tell
Twirl heads Peal laughter
Love comes after
Love for whom
Love for me

Love for me

SONG OF SONGS

In your arms I passed the other half of life

. . .

When on the first day God put the word for each thing
             between the teeth of Adam
Your name dwelt on my tongue awaiting me
As winter awaits the birth of roses

. . .

      O lips like a swallow

. . .

I am as him who came on the hill
And took a partridge in his hand by chance
And there he stands bewildered by his fortune
Ah how soft are the feathers and the fear that beats in its heart

. . .

      Do not speak to me of the sea
      To me who all my life
          has sung to you
      Do not speak to me of my mother
      To me who all my life
          has clung to you

. . .

      In a flash the masked form
      Of your face turns away from me
      Your step your voice all is gone
      All is a missed opportunity

. . .

      Triumphant knowledge stated
      As dual mystery
      My wife without end I created
      In the world which created me

LOVE OF ELSA

Jealous of the drops of rain
Every drop too like a kiss
Eyes that shine and shine again
Reasons for my jealousness

Jealous jealous of all mirrors
Of the sting of honey bees
Of forgetting of remembering
Of abandonment in sleep

Of the pavement that she chooses
Of the rustling of the breeze
Ever-living jealousy
Wakes me even when I dream

Jealous of a song or cry
Of the slightest breath or sigh
Jealous of the hyacinths
Of a scent a memory

Jealous jealous of the statues
With their vacant baleful looks
Jealous jealous when she's silent
Jealous of her white-paged books

Of a shiver in mid-winter
Of a laugh a word of praise
Of the trees new-green in springtime
Of the changes in her dress

Of the clutch of clinging brier
Of her love of warmth and fire
And at morning and at midnight
Of the comb that combs her hair

Of the friends she makes at random
Why she wears her turquoises
Stealthy shadows sly and noiseless
Make my nights a martyrdom

Jealous of each month and season
Nails by thousands prick and wound
Lacking sense and lacking reason
Jealous as a jealous hound

Jealous when she's late arriving
Jealous when she's here at last
All her actions are surprising
Jealous jealous of guitars

YOU LEFT ME

You left me by all doors
You left me in all deserts
I looked for you at dawn I lost you at noon
You were nowhere when I came
I knew my room would be Sahara without you
A sunday crowd where no-one was like you
A day more desolate than a jetty pointing toward the sea
All is Silent and you do not answer me

You left me here motionless
You left me everywhere you took away my eyes
From the heart of dreams
You left me like an unfinished sentence
An object of chance a thing a chair
A visitor at summer's ending
A postcard in a drawer
All my life fell from you and little did you care

You never saw me cry you turned your head away
At the sight of my grief
With a sigh in which I had no place

Did you never feel pity for the shadow at your feet

A VERY SMALL CHAGALL...

A very small Chagall comprising the universe
With colour and perspective and everything provided
Painting all askew and the canvas in reverse
And far too many people all lop-sided
The guests look hungry and just a trifle silly
Nothing quite ready and the table needs setting
Send the horse to the grocers to fetch some roses
A very small Chagall eyes larger than the belly
A very small Chagall like a wedding
A stray violinist from somewhere in the neighbourhood
A very small Chagall forgotten in a mirror
A very small Chagall looking rather good in a blue sunday suit
                    with some orange near the ear
A very small Chagall with lovers on the roof
I've lost the ring and gloves whatever shall I do
For the key to the picture eludes me too
Besides the guests have left and they haven't seen the bride

Such a very small Chagall
                    but I'm hanged if I know where to hang it

Yves Bonnefoy

(Tours 1923–   )

Poet and translator. His first published poems (*Du mouvement et de l'immobilité de Douvre*, 1953) shewed at once an exceptional gift for combining contemporary expression with lyric felicity. He has since published two collections (*Hier régnant désert*, 1960; *Pierre écrit*, 1965) and a fine translation of *Hamlet*.

BATTLEGROUND

1

Here in defeat is the warrior of mourning,
While he kept watch by the fountain, see
I waken (and this is because of the trees
and the sound of the waters) and yet still dream.

He is silent. His face is the countenance
I seek in all fountains and cliffs, dead brother.
Face of the night, now past and vanquished,
Bent on the tattered shoulders of the dawn.

He is silent. How can he say at the battle's end
Who was the victor, what use for speech?
He bows his defenceless head to the ground,
His sole desire to die, to die his last relief.

2

But does he weep beside a deeper fountain
And does he flourish, dahlia of the dead,
In the sanctuary of November's turgid waters
That surge towards us loud as a dying world?

To me it seems, crouched on the hard dawning
Of this day which is my due and I have conquered,
That I hear sobbing the eternal presence
Of my secret demon, secret unburied still.

O you will come again, shore of my strength!
But let it be despite this day which guides me.
Shadows, you are no more. If shadows be reborn
Then that will be at night because of the night.

HIC EST LOCUS PATRIAE

The sky too low for you was rent asunder,
Trees encroached the limits of your blood.
So other armies came, Cassandra,
And nothing could survive their amorous flood.

A marble vase adorned the threshold. Poised
Against it smiled the one who had returned.
So sank the sun upon 'The Place of Trees',
That was a day of words, a night of wind.

Joë Bousquet

(NARBONNE 1897–CARCASSONNE 1950)

Poet, critic, essayist, novelist. Severely wounded at the age of seventeen in the first world war, Bousquet was bedridden for the rest of his life—a life of incessant pain borne with great courage and philosophy, qualities which are reflected in his writings (*Il ne fait pas assez noir*, 1932; *Traduit du silence*, 1941; *La Neige d'un autre âge*, 1952; etc.).

SOWN PATHS

Is it life or the wind
Unwinding its spindle
Of silver and grass in the spring?

Day's gifts to the absent
Remembered in dying!

Childhood was but a few hours
To the wandering mind
Encircled by dreams—
Its shadows are ours.

—Spinning-wheel, sower of paths
Revolving with earth,
Grind the organ of grief.

And the mill-wheel grinds
A thread of fine sand
For the river to spin;

Grinds, in the forest wheel
And the suffering leaf,
The thread of our sorrows.

This is the way of a song
For the voice that is tuned!
Spin the torturing wheel,
Nothing is naught but wrong.

—Bells of blood we hear
Struck with the fist of dawn;
What hand has bound you
To the wheel of the years?

—A hand that demands
Return to the thread of day;
The stone that grinds the bread
As the water flows
To the mill to pray
To be saved from the wave—
The bird that flies without wings.

—Water of silver, of bells,
Where are the wings of the bird?

In the steam from the oxen's flanks,
The wings are between.

From the flying day that I want,
Where do they drag the plough?

Between the oxen's horns
To the heart of the furrowed stones.

—I cannot see the furrow
Under the hoof; a goat
Has grazed—It has gone
With the grass on the roof.

If you hear then you see it
Spinning on wheels of rain,
Linking yourself to those that remain,
And you tell how once on a time
A fool wept for heart-ache—
King he became by mistake.

THE BURDEN OF BLACK

All snow is the image
Of evil unknown,
A fête and a marriage
Where day feasts alone.

In every decade,
Though men come and go
Unaware of its lack,
A white poppy will grow.

In my mother's garden
Flowers come as they may,
My eyelids are closed
On deceitful day.

Where are the colours
That shone for the night?
Red sheds its wings
And cold kills the white.

On ice-frozen lips
Is a dead butterfly;
From shadow to shadow
Our love has passed by.

Open your eyes
And forget your sad folly
That doubts the existence
Of the white poppy.

Your name counts for nothing,
That is its secret,
It shivers as black
As flowers in a thicket.

From ice pluck the blossom;
Night sees from afar
A glimmer that passes . . .
Is that what you are?

André Breton

(Tinchebray, Orne, 1896–Paris 1966)

Poet and prose writer. One of the most colourful and controversial personalities in contemporary literature. Initially influenced by Paul Valéry, during his war service he became interested, through the works of Freud, in the subconscious mind, and after a short period in which he was involved in the *dada* group, he launched his remarkable *Le Manifeste du Surréalisme*, 1924. The influence of his work on the literature and art of this century cannot be over-estimated. (*Nadja*, 1928; *L'Union libre*, 1931; *L'Amour fou*, 1937; *Poèmes*, 1948.)

ON THE ROAD TO SAN ROMANO

Poetry comes in bed like love is made
Crumpled sheets are the dawn of things
Poetry comes in bed

It has all the space it requires
The first not the last conditions it

> Bird's-eye view of a kite
> Dew on a horsetail
> Thought of a bottle of Traminer misty
> > served on a silver salver
> Rod of tourmaline tall by the sea
> And the route of mental adventure
> Rising high to
> A halt that is suddenly choked with undergrowth

It does not shout from the roof-tops
Mistaken to leave the door open
Or call for witnesses
Shoals of fish and hedges of tits
Rails at the start of a railway station
Reflections from either bank
Grooves in the bread
Bubbles on a brook
Calendar days
St. John's wort
The act of love and the act of poetry
Are incompatible
With reading aloud a daily paper

       The feel of the sun's rays
       The blue glint that sparks from a woodman's
           axe
       A stag-beetle's filament formed like a heart or a
           noose
       The measured beat of beavers'
           tails
       The speed of lightning
       Spurt of iced almonds from far-distant limits
       Avalanche

The best bedchamber
No gentlemen not the eighth Chamber
Nor reek of a barracks on sunday night

       Dance formations wheeling half-naked
           above the tides
       A woman's body against a wall outlined
           in stabbing thrusts
       Clear clouds of smoke
       Curls of your hair
       Curves of a Philippine sponge
       Coils of a coral serpent
       Entry of ivy into the ruins
       All time is before it

Poetic orgasm like the love-grip of flesh
While it endures
Keeps out of sight all the world's sorrows

THEY TELL ME THAT THE SANDS ...

They tell me that the sands out there are black
With lava flowing to the sea
Converging on the base of some proud peak
         smoke-wreathed in snow
What then is this far distant land
Which seems to draw all light from your life-blood
It trembles vivid on your eyelids' fringe
Soft to your flesh like immaterial linen
Fresh from the trunk of ages still half-open
Behind you
Casting its last dark fires between your legs
The earth of long-lost paradise
Glass of shadows mirror of love
And yet lower close to your arms outstretched
For proof of Spring's assertion
SIC
That sin does not exist
All the ocean's apple-tree in flower

FREE LOVE

My love with hair like a wood fire
With hints of sheet-lightning
And the shape of an hour-glass
My love with the shape of an otter gripped in a tiger's jaws
My love with lips like a crest or a cluster of stars from the ultimate
    galaxy
With teeth like the prints of white mice on the snow-white earth
With amber tongue like a polished wine-glass
My love with the tongue of a sacrament stabbed to the heart
With the tongue of a doll that opens and shuts its eyes
With the tongue of a fabulous gem
My love with lashes like children's pencils
With brows like the brim of a swallow's nest
My love with temples like the slated roof of a green-house
And mist on the windows
My love with shoulders of champagne
And a fountain of dolphins' heads frozen in ice
My love with wrists like matches
My love with fingers of chance and the ace of hearts
With fingers like new-mown hay
My love with arm-pits of sable and beech-mast
On the eve of Saint John
Like nests in a hedge of privet
With arms of sea-foam and sluices
And a mixture of wheat from the mill
My love with legs like spindles
With the movement of clockwork and hopeless grief
My love with calves like an elder-tree's pith
My love with feet like initials
With feet like bunches of keys with feet like seals of molten wax
My love with neck of pearl barley
With throat of the Golden Valley
And a tryst in the bed of the torrent
With breasts of night
My love with breasts of ocean mole-hills
With breasts where a cresset flames with rubies

With the Rose Spectre's breasts drenched in dew
My love with belly fan-shaped in daylight
With belly of giant claw
My love with a bird's back in vertical flight
With a back of quick silver
A back of light
With neck of turned stone and moist chalk
And the tilt of a glass drained of drink
My love with cockle-shell haunches
With haunches of lustre an arrow's flight
With a white peacock's quills
Of intangible weight
My love with seat of pleasures and amianthus
My love with seat like a swan's back
My love with the hind-parts of Spring
With the sex of an iris
My love with a sex like the mines of a platypus
With a sex like sea-weed and ancient sweetmeats
My love with a sex like a mirror
My love with eyes full of tears
With eyes like a violet panoply and a magnetic needle
My love with eyes like the prairie
My love with eyes of water to drink in prison
My love with eyes like wood still under the axe
With eyes at the level of water at the level of air of earth and fire

SOONER LIFE

Sooner life than these thin prisms although
                    their colours are purer
Sooner than this still dark hour than these
                    awful wagons of cold flame
Than these over-ripe stones
Than this latched heart
Than this murmuring tide
Than this dead-white stuff singing at once
                    in air and on land
Than this nuptial blessing which binds my brow
                    to total vanity
          Sooner life

Sooner life with its draped provocations
Its scars of evasions
Sooner life than a rose-window on my tomb
Life to be faced and always before us
Where a voice cries Are you there where another replies Are you there
Alas I am scarcely there
And yet the game with death is due
                    to be played
          Sooner life

Sooner life sooner respectable Childhood
The ribbon cast by a fakir
Resembles the sliding-rule of the world
The sun has beauty doomed to be wrecked
If only the woman's body is like it
You dream contemplating the whole long stretch
Or simply when closing your eyes to the glorious storm
                    called your hand
          Sooner life

Sooner life waiting in waiting-rooms
When you know you will never go in
Sooner life than these thermal hostels
Where service is grudgingly given

Sooner life long and uncomfortable
Here where books on shelves shut themselves
                                    less gently
          Sooner life

Sooner life as a ground of contempt
For this passably beautiful head
As antidote to that perfection it names
                              yet it fears
Life the mask of God
Life like a virgin passport
A little town like Pont-à-Mousson
And when all's said and done
          Sooner life

René Guy Cadou

(SAINTE-REINE-DE-BRETAGNE 1920–LOUISFERT 1951)

Poet and novelist. His first poems were published at the
early age of seventeen (*Brancardiers de l'aube*, 1937)
when he was strongly influenced by the work of Pierre
Reverdy. His later poems (*La Vie rêvée*, 1944; *Pleine
Poitrine*, 1946, and *Les Biens de ce monde*, 1951) are
works of distinct originality, combining sentiment and
lyricism with immaculate taste. His premature death was
a great loss to French poetry.

HE WHO ENTERS...

He who enters by chance a poet's house
Little knows that its furniture has such power
That each knot of wood cages more
Cries of birds than the entire forest's heart
It is enough for a lamp to place its woman's throat
At nightfall against a polished angle
Suddenly to free a thousand hosts of bees
And the new-bread scent of flowering cherries
For such is the happiness of this solitude
That a stroke with the palm of the hand
Transmutes this heavy furniture so dark and secret
To the feather-lightness of a tree at morning

FOUR LOVE POEMS FOR HELEN

I

Like a river that begins
To love its journeying
You found yourself one day
All naked in my arms

One thought alone I had
To cover you with leaves
With leaves and my bare hands
To keep you safe and warm

How other could I love you
If not through living waters
Woman's body clinging
A moment to my fingers

How other could I look
At you while you were lying
On all those sun-warm stones
If not with new desire?

Maiden you answer best
This obscure question
By enduring the soft
Pressure of my heart on yours

And if your heart still fears
This transformation
Remember that your love
I love more than your self.

II

I waited for you just as one waits for ships
In the years of dryness when the corn
Grows no higher than an ear in the grass
That listens frightened to the great voice of time

I waited for you and all the quays all the roads
Resounded with burning steps which went
Towards you already borne upon my shoulders
Like a gentle rain that never dies

You did not move except your eyelids fluttered
Like birds' feet on frosted windows
I did not see you save in this solitude
Which placed its leaf-like hands about my neck

But this was you in the light of my life
The loud morning noise that roused me
All my birds all my vessels all my countries
Those stars those millions of stars that awoke

Ah how well you spoke when all the windows
Sparkled in the night just like new wine
When doors opened on airy cities
Where we went embracing through the streets

You came so far behind your countenance
That I no longer knew if each lone beat
Of my heart would last until that time
When you would be stronger in me than my blood

III

The horses of love tell of encounters
Made while pursuing deserted ways
A woman unknown detains them her eyes
Charged with grief and the darkness of forests

Be careful they say for her sorrow is ours
And you who have suffered the pangs of love
Will wander no more bare-headed beneath
The trees unaware of the burden of life

But I roam and I know that your hands respond
In the shallow pretence of gathering flowers
And you do not expect to solder our souls
By lovingly carving our christian names

As green apples ripen from sun to sun
You finger your cheeks that are grey with time
And you shield your eyes weary of town
With a film of sleep in the forest of dreams

Show me your breasts let me see in heaped snow
The beast of the glaciers crowned with twin
Circles of day and the joy of existence
Untamed and eyes that are soft but profound

So you seemed to me my love when you came
Like a stricken tree in the summer heat
Like a sweet temptation that lasted
A second and all eternity

IV

Behind the curtains and the thickness of time
How cold the nights are without you my child

Sleep and street are crowded with people who chatter
Aloud and when I call you everything shatters

In spite of all this I call to you and I know
That in spite of these heart-beats you will return

Creating again the grace of your hands
And the breath of the winds rekindle your face

This I can see in the thickness of time
Like a flame that is living still my child

DECEMBER NIGHT

O friends with your news where are you tonight
In what niche of my life so long untouched?
Quietly I should like to make you understand
This minute movement of grass in my hands
Searching for you in darkness under the level
Waters of day, beside the banks of destiny!
In the drear waters of my sadness, silted
In this mill-race of sweetness where nothing counts
Any more except a few drops of purest rain like tears?
Forgive me for loving you in spite of myself
For losing you ceaselessly in the crowd
O criers of intimate papers, sole prophets
Sole friends in this world and the next.

Blaise Cendrars

(La Chaux-de-fonds 1887–Paris 1961)

Poet, novelist and adventurer. A prolific writer with an enormous enthusiasm for life and an insatiable urge to travel to remote places of the globe. Severely wounded in the first world war, the loss of his right arm did not prevent him from big-game hunting in Africa or exploring the Amazon, or from joining the British Army in 1939 as a war correspondent. He was equally adventurous in his poetry (*La Prose du Transsibérien et de la Petite Jehanne de France*, 1913; *Profond Aujourd'hui*, 1917; *Kodak*, 1924). After *Kodak* Cendrars abandoned poetry for the novel.

ISLANDS

1. *Victuals*

The little port is very lively this morning
Coolies – Tagals Chinese Malays – busily discharging a great junk with
    gilded poop and sails of plaited bamboo
The cargo composed of china from the great island of Nippon
Swallow's nests gathered in the caves of Sumatra
Sea-slugs
Preserved ginger
Bamboo shoots pickled in vinegar
All the traders are in a flutter
Mr Noghi ostentatiously dressed in a check suit of American
    manufacture speaks very fluent English
It is in this language that he engages in discussions with these
    gentlemen
Japanese Kanakas Tahitians Papuans Maoris and Fijians

2. *Prospectus*

Visit our island
It is the most southerly of Japanese possessions
Our country is certainly too little known in Europe
It merits bringing to the attention
The flora and fauna are very varied and have hardly been studied to
     date
In fact you will find everywhere picturesque points of view
And in the interior
Ruins of Buddhist temples which are of their kind pure marvels

3. *The Viper with the Red Crest*

With the aid of a syringe Pravaz practises several injections with
     Doctor Yersin's serum
Then he enlarges the wound in the arm by trying a crucial incision
     with a scalpel
It makes the wound bleed
Then he cauterizes it with a few drops of hypochloride of lime

4. *Japanese House*

Bamboo poles
Flimsy planks
Paper stretched on frames
There is no provision for any serious heating

5. *Little Garden*

Chrysanthemums
Cycas and bananas
Flowering cherries
Orange palms and superb coco-trees loaded with fruit

6. *Grottos*

In a basin filled with Chinese goldfish and fish with monstrous jaws
Some of them wear little silver rings inserted in their gills

7. *Light and Subtle*

The air is fragrant
Musk amber and lime-tree flowers
The mere act of living is a sheer delight

8. *Keepsake*

The sky and the sea
Clouds come to caress the roots of the coco-trees and the great
    tamarinds with metallic foliage

9. *Poisonous Creek*

The water is so transparent and still
One can see deep down below the white branches of coral
The prismatic swaying of suspended jelly-fish
The flights of yellow fish pink lilac
At the foot of the wavering sea-weed azure sea-slugs and sea-urchins
    green and violet

10. *Hatouara*

She has no knowledge of European styles
Her hair fuzzy and blue-black is piled *a la japonaise* and kept in place
    with coral pins
She is naked under her silk kimono
Naked up to the elbows

Firm lips
Languorous eyes
Straight nose
Flesh the colour of bright copper
Little breasts
Opulent buttocks

She possesses vivacity frankness of movement and gesture
The youthful look of a charming animal

Her science: the grammar of poise
She swims as one writes a novel of 400 pages
Indefatigable
Haughty
Easily
Lovely sustained prose
She catches some tiny fish which she puts in the hollow of her mouth
Then she dives fearlessly
She glides between the coral and the polychromatic sea-wrack
Soon to reappear at the surface

37

Smiling
Holding in her hands two fat goldfish with silver bellies

Very proud of a new blue silk dress of her gold embroidered slippers
    of a pretty coral necklace which someone has just given her this
    morning
She brings me a basket of fantastic spiny crabs and those enormous
    tropical sea shrimps we call 'caracks' and which are as long as
    your hand

11. *La Dolce Vita*
Garden bushy as a glade
On the idle beach the eternal rustling song of the wind in the leaves of
    the filaos
Wearing a light straw hat armed with a large paper parasol
I watch the play of the seagulls and cormorants
Or I examine a flower
Or some stone
With each movement I scare the squirrels and the palmetto rats

Through the open window I see the elongated hull of a steamer of
    medium tonnage
Anchored about two kilometres from the coast and surrounded
    already by junks sampans and boats loaded with local
    merchandise
At last the sun is setting
The air has a crystalline purity
The same nightingales sing full-throatedly
And the big vampire bats move silently across the moon on velvet
    wings

A young girl completely nude passes by
Her head is covered with one of those ancient hats which are today
    the joy of collectors
She holds in her hand a large bunch of pale flowers their penetrating
    scent recalls both the tuberose and narcissus
She stops short in front of the garden door
Some phosphorescent flies settle on the cone that crowns her hat
    adding yet more to its weird appearance

Nocturnal noises
Dead branches that creak
Creepings crawlings
Insect rustlings
Birds in nests
Whispering voices
The giant plane-trees are pale grey in the moonlight
From the top of their arch trail slender lianas an invisible mouth
    sways them in the breeze
The stars melt like sugar

FETISHES

(Lines written in the British Museum)

1   A vein of hard wood
    Two embryonic arms
    The man tears at his belly
    And adores his erected virility

2   Who is threatening you
    You who slink off
    Hands on haunches
    Crouching
    Deflated?

3   Knot of wood
    Head shaped like a gland
    Hard and stubborn
    Bare-faced smooth
    Young unsexed god cynically bland

4   Envy has gnawed at your chin
    You are cheated by greed
    You redress
    All that your face is lacking
    By making yourself geometric
    Arborescent
    Adolescent

5   See the man and the woman
Equally ugly equally naked
He's not as fat as she but strong as an ox
Hands on stomach and mouth like a money-box

6   She
The bread of her sex which she bakes three times a day
And the taut skin of her belly
Drag
At the neck and shoulders

7   I am ugly!
Through snuffling the smell of girls
My head swells in my solitude and my nose
Is about to drop off

8   I wanted to fly from the wives of the chieftain
My head shattered by the stone of the sun
In the sands
All that is left is my mouth
Open like my mother's womb
Crying

9   He
Who is bald
Has only a mouth
A member dangling down to his knees
And feet cut off

10   See the woman I like the most
Two sharp wrinkles flanking wondering lips
A blue brow
White at the temples
And a look like polished brass.

René Char

(L'Isle-sur-la-Sorgue 1907–   )

A member of the surrealists before the war (*Le Marteau sans maître*, 1934), his experiences as a Resistance fighter in the *maquis* profoundly affected his subsequent writing. His poetry, though sometimes obscure, is deeply felt and often very moving (*Les Feuillets d'Hypnos*, 1946; *Fureur et mystère*, 1948; *Les Paysans*, 1949). Char's work has had considerable influence on contemporary French poetry.

MADELEINE TO THE NIGHTLIGHT
(after a painting by Georges de La Tour)

   Today I wish the grass could be white to blot out the evidence of seeing you suffer: I shall not look beneath your hand so young in shape and firm, lacking the pargetting of the dead. One day discreetly, from others less eager than I, I shall remove your linen chemise, and take possession of your alcove. But, on leaving, they will forget to dowse the nightlight and a little of the oil will spill through the dagger of the flame upon the impossible solution.

DONNERBACH MUHLE
Winter 1939

November mists, the bell tolls in the woods, from the last track to be crossed tonight, and disappears;
    the distant wish of the wind to separate return to steel from the leave that is ending.
    Seasons of docile beasts, of guileless girls, you retain powers that my own power contradicts; you possess the eyes of my name, this name they ask me to forget.
    Knell of a world loved too much, I hear monsters trample an unsmiling earth. My scarlet sister sweats. My maddened sister calls to arms.
    The lake moon sets on the shore where the sweet vegetal fire of summer falls on the waves which tug it towards a bed of deep cinders.
        Traced by the guns
        —to live, limit immense—
        The house in the forest is aglow with light:
        Thunder, the stream, the mill.

IN A STATE OF BELLIGERENCE
(1943)

Our Lady of Light, staying aloof on your rock, embroiled with your church, patronizing its rebels, we can do nothing but gaze at you from below.

Sometimes I hated you. You were never naked. Your mouth was unclean. But today I know I exaggerated because those who kissed you had polluted their food.

Wayfarers that we are we have only asked to rest before exhaustion. Protectress of our efforts, you are untouched save by the particle of love that clothes you.

You are the moment of an enlightened lie, the crusted cudgel, the punitive lamp. I am hot-headed enough to tear you to pieces or take your hand. You are defenceless.

Too many rogues watch you and see your fear. You have no choice but complicity. The utter disgust in building for them, in working to repay their devoted service.

I have broken my silence now all have departed and you have nothing left except this pinewood. Ah! run to the road, make friends, become child-hearted beneath the lowering clouds.

The world has spun so far since your coming, that it is nothing but a bag of bones, a lust for cruelty. O swooning Lady, servant of chance, your light is restored when the famished see it.

GIVE BACK TO THEM...

Give back to them that which is no longer theirs,
They shall see the harvest grain imprisoned
In the ears of corn and stirring in the grass.
Teach them, from fall to flight, the twelve months
            of their countenance,
They shall cherish the void in their hearts till desire
            ensues;
For nothing is made for wreck or rejoices in ashes;
And who knows, seeing the earth swell to fruition,
If aught can check the riot though all is lost.

PYRENEES

Mountains of the deluded great,
Upon your fervid towers' topmost height
The last light flickers out.

Nothing but emptiness and avalanche,
Distress and regret!

All those lovelorn troubadours
Watched their gentle pessimistic realm
Whiten with one summer's passing.

Ah! snow is relentless,
Wanting us to suffer at its feet,
Wanting us to die a frozen death
When we have sojourned in the sands.

THE SWIFT

The swift with wings too wide, who twists and cries its joy round the housetops. Such is the heart.

It withers the thunder. It scatters its seed in the tranquil sky. If it touches the ground, it shatters.

Its retort is the swallow, which abhors the familiar. What use is the filligree tower?
It poises in the darkest hollow. Nothing it tries is too narrow.

In the long light of summer, it darts in the shadows through shutters of midnight.

No eye can follow its flight. Its cry is its whole being. It swoops swift as an arrow.
Such is the heart.

Paul Claudel

(Villeneuve-sur-Fère 1868–Paris 1955)

Poet, dramatist, essayist and diplomat. One of the out-
standing poets of France, Claudel was a devout catholic
and his deeply religious feelings are often reflected in
his poetry. The Claudel 'verset' indeed has its origin in
biblical verse and he uses it to magnificent effect in
his long epic poems (*Cinq Grandes Odes*, 1910). Claudel
had a distinguished diplomatic career and served as
ambassador in Tokyo, Washington and Brussels. His
work is too important to cover in this brief introduction
(but one must mention at least two of his celebrated
stage works: *L'Annonce faite à Marie*, 1912 and *Le
Soulier de satin*, 1930). The short poems included in
this anthology one hopes will stimulate the reader to
explore his more important works.

AUTUMN SONG

In the bright autumnal light
    Of morning we departed.
The magnificence of this autumn
    Thundered in the distant sky,

All day the morning lasted,
    A day of virgin silver,
A day of golden air until the hour Diana
    Raised her crescent in the azure night.

A day entire of silver, and the forest—
    One great angel clothed in gold.
An angel rimmed with red, each tree
    Burning fire on flame and gold on gold.

O the scent of the dying forest—smell it!
O the smell of the smoke—scent it! and living blood with death
blended!
O the immense suspense of glittering gold seen through the clear rose
of glowing day!
O colour of the gillyflowers!

Now silent, now resounding, now muffled, now itself regaining,
Within the forest's heart I hear,
Advancing now and now refraining, a sound prolonged and sombre,
The horn's remote inimitable call.

The dark call of the horn, disconsolate,
Because of time that is no more,
That is no more because of this most glorious day,
Through this alone it is no more.

A time, alas,
A time no more to be:
Because of the gold that I behold,
Because of the gold for ever gone,
Because of the twilight I behold!
Because of the night that I behold!
Because of the moon and the stars' Great Bear that I behold.

THE WAY TO THE CROSS
ELEVENTH STATION

Behold! God is no longer with us. He is cast to the ground.
The pack in full cry have seized him like a stag in the grip of the hounds.
You are truly ours, Lord! You have come to us at last!
They held you down, they held you, their knee upon your heart.
This hand is God's right hand, this hand the hangman rends.
They bind the Lamb by the feet, they fasten Omnipotence.

46

With chalk they inscribe his title, his regal name and race,
And when he tastes the bitterness, then we shall see his face.

Eternal Son for whom the universe alone is your Infinity,
See then with us this narrow place coveted by Divinity!
Behold Elias out-stretched upon his death-bed,
Behold the Glory of Solomon and the royal throne of David,
Behold this strong unyielding cross our love-gift where he lies!
It is difficult for a God to shrink to human size.
They tug, and the shattered body cries out and cracks and smarts,
He is clamped down like a wine-press, he is fearfully dragged apart.
The words of the Prophet have come to pass, their truth at last is shown:
  They have pierced my hands and feet. They have numbered all my bones.

You are taken, Lord, there is no retreat.
You are nailed to the cross by the hands and feet.
I need no longer search the heavens with heretics and fools.
This God alone is enough for me secure between four nails.

LINES WRITTEN IN EXILE
(fragment)

Pilgrim, no more remains for me except the way
By which I came, on which I go, passing, tomorrow
Yesterday, fields or woods, flat valley or steep hill,
The stream that follows me and stretches far ahead,
Nothing more the marcher's stoic heart sustains
But this—the narrow road on which his footsteps stride
To a ceaseless rhythm that impels him on.
In vain, though now to gentle softness cooled, the air
Enfolds him (while in the wide expanse of autumn sky
A charnel scent exhales from leaves beneath my feet,
Less strong, O heart, than these my bitter roses!)
Behind me darkness and before me roseate light,
Although my shadow grows then wanes with ebbing day
My steps will neither pace less firm nor will they falter.

47

The silence is profound, the landscape void,
No more remains for me except this solid road
And, to one proud traveller, the most sweet presence
Of a sunset where dawn embraces night.

Robert Desnos

(PARIS 1900–CZECHOSLOVAKIA 1945)

One of the leaders of the surrealist movement (*Corps et Bien*, collected poems published in 1930). During the German occupation Desnos was a member of a Resistance network. Arrested by the Gestapo in 1944 he was sent to various notorious concentration camps— Fresnes, Compiègne, Buchenwald and Auschwitz— finally dying of typhus and starvation in a *stalag* in Czechoslovakia shortly after its liberation by the Russian army. His last and most moving poem was composed for his wife Youki just before he died.

DON JUAN'S TOWN

Limping, lurching went the blind,
The crippled, the humpbacked, the goitrous,
The constables, drunks and the loiterers.

And fog, breathed on café windows,
Caused a hundred ships to sink;
Seven o'clock sirens said to them all: It's time for a drink.

Don Juan stopped at a spot
Where I know there's a fountain,
A fire alarm and a barrow secured by a chain.

Till midnight he stayed
Without getting jaded
Or bored, alone with his thoughts.

At midnight a woman in mourning,
Naked beneath the crêpe adorning
Her hat, came round the street corner.

She brought him a bottle of wine and a glass,
She brought him a dead bird's carcase,
She gave him the bird and a glass of red wine.

Then suddenly out of a doorway leapt
A tiny girl with adorable legs,
She gave him her doll and a black bead necklace.

In a lighted window a woman undressed;
As she took off her clothes she threw them
Down at the feet of Don Juan.

From a flower stall in the square
A woman brought him a rose,
And a newspaper seller all the papers that she could spare.

A lady, lovely but hateful,
Showed him her watch,
And said: It no longer goes.

From a neighbouring shop a woman in clogs
Wrapt a fish in her apron,
A fish like nothing on earth.

She threw the fish in the gutter
And there it spluttered
Till at last—came Death.

LINES ON A SUMMER PAVEMENT

Let us sit by the roadside,
Warmed by the sun, washed by the sun
In the fine reek of dust
From a day's work done.
Before night comes,
Before the first street lamp is lit,
We shall see in the gutter
The mirror of clouds from afar
Spilling their blood on distant horizons,
And, above the roofs, the birth of a star.

10 JUNE 1936

At the turn of the road
He stretched out his hand
To welcome the day.

The sky was so clear
That the clouds in the air
Were like foam on the sea.

And apple-tree blossom
Was white as the washing
That hung by the well.

The song of the spring
Was the song of life passing
By valley and fell.

And far in the forest
Where grass is the greenest
The air was humming
With sounds like a bell.

Life was so sweet
It entered so deep in his eyes
And his ears and his heart

That he laughed out loud:
He laughed at the world and the sighs
Of the wind in the flowering trees,

He laughed at the smell of the earth,
He laughed at the clean linen drying
He laughed at the clouds that sailed through the sky.

As he laughed
A girl with the face of beauty
Came out of the house nearby.

And the girl laughed too,
And when her laugh ended
The birds sang anew.

She laughed to see him laugh
And the doves preening their feathers
By the well of still waters
Heard the sound of her laughter
Die in the air.

Never to meet again.

She went often that way
Where the man stretched his hand
In delight at the day.

He thought often of her
And the light of her face
Shone bright in his eyes.

She thought often of him
And the light of his face shone again
In the well where still water lies.

And one by one,
Pale as playing cards dealt at dawn,
The years pass by.

They rot under ground
And honest worms eat them
And earth fills their mouths
To stop them from speaking.

Perhaps in the night they call to each other
If death does not smother the sound
Of their cries,
For death has a horror of noise.

The years go by but the road remains.

And every day the world new-born
Comes like an egg at dawn
To the wayfarer passing that way.

And every day the sky is so clear
That the clouds in the air
Are like foam on the sea.

Dead! Poor outcasts
Each in your cell,
We hear your grief
And the tale you tell.

We live, we swim
Through each lovely year
For life is good and the air is pure.

LANDSCAPE

I dreamed of love, and love is still my dream;
But love no more is lilac wreathed in roses
Burdening with scent the forest where reposes
At the path's untwisted end a burning flame.

I dreamed of love, and love is still my dream;
But love no more is lightning launched by storms
That darts its fire on castles, wrecks, deforms,
Flashing a swift farewell to the tumbled scene.

It is the flint sparked by footsteps in the night,
The word no learned lexicon can cite,
The white sea-foam, the heaped clouds in the sky.

In growing old all becomes hard and clots,
Roads without names and cords without the knots;
I am a landscape stiff with paint—and dry.

THE HARVEST

Incredible to believe
We live, we think, we breathe;
Incredible to believe
In death, defunct, divorced from time;
Incredible to believe
And more incredible seems
Our belief in memory and dreams,
A body lacking mind.

Sweet roses of the past,
Roses, sweet-scented roses,
Forlorn and shivering in the dawn;
Night so quickly closes
On your sad fate—its length and pace
So like our own life's span
As if we brought you faded
To show in some Salon.

Your gods were far too fragile,
Too minute, striving till late to earn,
Each in his tiny domicile,
A living in return.
Much greater is our fortune,
More sombre is our fate,
We do not want the moon,
We do not fear death.

LINES ON THE RUE SAINT-MARTIN
(1942)

I do not like the Rue Saint-Martin
Now that André Platard's gone,
I do not like the Rue Saint-Martin,
Wine is sour when you drink alone.

I do not like the Rue Saint-Martin
Now that André Platard's gone.
He's my friend, he's my chum,
We shared our bread, we shared a room,
In the Rue Saint-Martin—no more fun.

He's my friend, he's my chum,
He went before the rising sun.
They took him away and that was the end
And he hasn't been heard of by anyone
In the Rue Saint-Martin.

You can spare your breath, no use to pray
To Saint Merri or Martin or Jacques or Gervais
Or Valèrien over the hill.
Time goes by and we know nothing still.
André Platard has gone
From the Rue Saint-Martin.

IN TIME OF DUNGEONS
(1942)

Have you already lost the password?
The castle forms a prison grim and black,
Beauty sings upon the ramparts,
The captive moans upon the rack.
Will you find the way again, the plain,
The spring, the shelter in the forest's heart,

The winding river when the dawn appears,
The full moon and the evening star?
A serpent darts towards the man,
Lacing its coils around him one by one,
Beauty sighs upon the rampart's edge,
Lances glitter in the setting sun.
Time with no return spurts at the man,
Enlaces him and twines about his throat,
O loves! O seasons! O faded beauties!
Coiled serpents shadowed in the undergrowth.

EPITAPH

(Lines written in a concentration camp. 1944)

I was alive in these forgotten times and have been dead
A thousand years. I lived enclosed but did not bow my head.
All human dignity was kept in bond
But I was free among blind slaves.

I was alive in these forgotten times but I was free;
I watched the waters and the earth and sky
Revolve around me, keeping to their ways,
And Seasons provide their honey and their birds.

You who are living yet and read these words
                    what have you done?
Do you regret the time I fought and strived?
Have you harvested in the common cause?
Have you enriched the town in which I lived?

O living men, fear nought of me for I am dead
                    and gone.
Nothing survives of this poor mind or corpse.

LAND OF COMPIÈGNE
(1944)

Chorus (*very quickly as if riding on horseback*)
> Chalk and flint and grass and chalk and flint
> And flint and dust and chalk and flint
> Grass, grass and flint, flint and chalk
>> (*rallentando*)
> Flint, flint and chalk
> And chalk and flint
> And chalk . . .

A voice
> Somewhere between l'Hay-les-Roses
> And Bourg-la-Reine and Antony
> Between the roses of l'Hay
> Between Clamart and Antony

Chorus (*very rhythmic*)
> Chalk and flint—chalk and flint
> And chalk
> And flint and chalk and flint and chalk
> And flint

A voice
> Between the roses of l'Hay
> And Clamart's trees
> Have you heard the siren sing
> The siren of Antony
> She who sang at Bourg-la-Reine
> And who still sings at Fresnes?

Chorus
> Land of Compiègne!
> Fertile earth yet sterile
> Earth of chalk and flint
> Within your flesh
> We mark the imprint of our steps
> So that one day the springtime rain
> Will there remain—a bird's eye
> Mirroring the sky, the Compiègne sky,
> With your stars and your scenes
> Heavy with memories and dreams

<pre>
                    Harder than flint
                    Softer than chalk beneath a knife

A voice   At Paris near to Bourg-la-Reine
                    I left my loves alone
                    Ah! let the sirens lull them.
                    My loves, I sleep so peacefully
                    And gather roses here at l'Hay
                    Which I shall bring you to one day
                    Heavy with perfumes and with dreams
                    And, like your eyelids, blooming
                    In the noontide of a life less brief
                    And full of flashes as a flint
                    And luminous as chalk

Chorus (alternating)
                    And chalk and flint and flint and chalk
                    Land of Compiègne!
                    Land made for walking
                    And for everlasting trees.
                    Land of Compiègne
                    Compares with all the lands on earth
                    Land of Compiègne!
                    One day we shall shed our dust
                    Upon your dust
                    And we shall leave you singing

A voice   We shall leave you singing
                    Singing to our loves
                    Time is short and life is brief

Another voice Nothing is more lovely than our loves

Another voice We shall leave our dust
                    In the dust of Compiègne
                              (scanned)
                    And we shall take away our loves
                    Our loves so it remembers us

Chorus   So it remembers us.
</pre>

THE CEMETERY
(1944)

Beneath these trees, and nowhere else, will be my tomb,
For here I picked the first spring leaves
Between a granite plinth and marble column.

I picked the first spring leaves
But other leaves will feed upon the happy putrefaction
Of this corpse which will live on
A hundred thousand years—if live it can.

But other leaves will feed upon the happy putrefaction,
And other leaves will blacken
Beneath the pen of those who write of thought and action.

And other leaves will blacken
With ink more fluid far than blood or water drawn from fountains,
Broken promises, or words cast beyond the mountains.

With ink more fluid far than blood or water drawn from fountains:
Can I defend my mind against oblivion,
Squirting sepia like a cuttle-fish and losing blood
                                    and losing breath?
Can I defend my mind against oblivion—and death?

NO, LOVE HAS NOT DIED...

No, love has not died within this heart or in these eyes,
Nor in this mouth whose lips proclaim the funeral rites begun.
        Listen, I have done
    with the picturesque with colours and with charm.
        Love I love, its sweetness and its cruelty,
        My love has but one name, one single form.
        All dies. Lips cling to lips
        My love has but one name, one form.
        And if some day you call to mind

59

A day at sea between America and France,
That moment when the sun's last rays danced
on the surface of the undulating waves, or yet that night the
storm drove us to shelter beneath a wayside tree, or speeding in a
sports-car,
Spring morning Boulevard Malesherbes,
A day of rain,
A dawn before you thought of sleep,
Say to yourself, I summoned your familiar ghost, that I
alone did love you most and that you did not know it to your
shame.
Say to yourself, such things need no regrets: Ronsard
before me and Baudelaire have sung the sorrows of old women
and the dead who scorned true love.
You, when you are dead
You will be lovely and entrancing still.
But I already will be dead, buried deep in your immortal
corpse, in your astounding image always there amid life's
wonders and eternity, but if I live
Your voice—its sounds, your glance—its gleam,
Your scent—the dear scent of your hair and much much
more will live in me,
In me who am no Baudelaire nor Ronsard,
In me whose name is Robert Desnos and who through
knowing you and loving you
Can look them in the face.
I, the said Robert Desnos, for love of you
Leave no request but this, that this alone
Shall be my true memorial
On this ungrateful earth.

I DREAMED SO MUCH OF YOU...

I dreamed so much of you that your reality is fading fast.

Is there still time to reach that living form and kiss those lips whence spring the voice so dear to me?

I dreamed so much of you that if I clasped your shade, my arms, so often folded on my breast, might fail perhaps to mould themselves to your sweet body's shape.

And, faced with the likelihood of dreams come true—a thought which haunts and governs me for days and years—I might perhaps become a shade myself.

O pendulum of feelings!

I dreamed so much of you that there is no more time perhaps to rouse myself. I sleep upright, my body bare to all appearances of life and love, and you alone who count for me today, although the brow and lips of anyone new-come are more accessible than yours.

I dreamed so much of you, walked so much and talked so much, lay with your ghost, that little more remains for me perhaps, save to be a ghost among all ghosts, a hundred times more shadow than the shade that moves, and still will move, so gladly on the sun-dial of your life.

THE LAST POEM

I dreamed so much of you
I walked so much, I talked so much,
Loved so much your shadow
That nothing more is left for me of you;
Save to be a shadow in the shadows,
To be a hundred times more shadow than a shadow,
To be a shadow who will come and come again
Into the sunshine of your life.

Marie-Jeanne Durry

(NEUILLY 1901–   )

Poet, essayist, dramatist, lecturer. At the moment
probably best known for her brilliant critical essays on
Stendhal, Chateaubriand, Flaubert and Jules Laforgue.
Poems include *Effacé*, 1954; *Soleils de sable*, 1958 and
the impressive *Mon Ombre*, 1962.

SUMMER

O road, O fields!
They were there
The man and the woman
In the sunlight,
No word no gesture
The tree, the soil.

You who remain to me
Beneath the black sky
Of memory,
In what chaste sleep
Without ripples
Did the world resolve?

THIS BLACK WORLD...

This black world which I enter
With eyes unbandaged,
Wide open that can see no more.

The way of shadow, the way of water
Caress the vanished grass, the obscure faces,
And glide about me, fading without
Eddies in the liquid night.

You stir so gently in my womb
Children of my youth
That your movements leave me with a feeling of wings.

Branches in the mist entwine,
I have passed before the isle and heard weapons,
Who called me from the shore? Who wept?
I have kept in my hands the traces of your tears.

I breathe the scent of buried forests,
O solid earth, blind and sub-marine!

I CAME INTO THE WORLD...

I came into the world with white hair,
Suffering I knew before my birth
And I dried your tears with trembling hands.
I know they flow to free the bonds I weave!
Perhaps at last death will be my youth?

HIDDEN SUN

The bird is no longer a bird, but an outline
Of winged flesh, skimming above the world.
The hill is no longer a hill but the veil of a thought.
With eyes closed I try to dream without shapes
Where the vaporous mind lives without living in daylight
And loses itself in a mist of faces.

STILL FURTHER

I have finished with the globe in four strides!
– Cast a hook in the sky!
Nothing more is needed but the sky
To fill your hands and melt within your mouth!
– I plunge in the flesh of the stars, I touch
Night with its long taste of grass, I couch
On the clouds of summer!
– Nothing more is needed but eternity.

THE SWIMMER

Asleep in silent water, O passer-by,
Prisoner of words which have not been uttered,
I dream in the depths of a well where all is inverted,
My eyelids are shuttered on sightless eyes;
The noonday sun strikes vainly at the waters,
Moving shadows swing beneath the surface,
I am further from life than a corpse.
All my secrets are sinking. I gnaw at my lips –
Lips which tremble with sleep and lost visions
And uncertain memories of speech.

What angler, leaning above with a magic net,
Would find in these depths of dark water
This voiceless song, this tangled shape
Among these water-flowers which are not corrollate,
This distant swimmer, hidden in her body
Of light, or captive and conquered, a soul asleep?
Catch me if you can, watcher who holds the net,
I float with arms outstretched like a cross of flesh.
Discover my dying reflections in these deeps,
Drag me from sleep, where my worlds are made
And unmade! If you haul me into the air
You will read my unveiled dreams upon my face.

Paul Eluard

(SAINT-DENIS 1895 – CHARENTON-LE-PONT 1952)

Paul Eluard was one of the founders of the surrealist movement. Among his major contributions to surrealism are: *Capitale de la douleur*, 1926, and *L'Amour la poésie*, 1929, still important for the exquisite sensitivity of his love poetry. Between the wars Eluard was probably the greatest single influence on French poetry. During the occupation he became a major figure in the Resistance and produced poems which, owing little to surrealism, have a strength and high purpose worthy of the cause he represented (*Poésie et Vérité*, 1942; *Au rendez-vous allemand*, 1944). His last years were saddened by the loss of his adored wife, Nusch (*Le Phénix*, 1952).

THE GERTRUDE HOFFMANN GIRLS

Gertrude, Dorothy, Mary, Claire, Alberta,
Charlotte, Dorothy, Ruth, Katie, Emma,
Louise, Peggy, Ferral, Harriet, Sara,
Florrie the nude, Maggie, Toots and Thelma,

Night-beauties, beauties-of-fire, beauties-of-rain,
Quivering breasts, flickering hands, wind-swept eyes
You show me the movements of light, you exchange
A frank stare for the glamour of spring,

Slender forms for a bunch of flowers,
Daring and dash for a spotless skin,
You barter love for a shiver of swords,
An easy laugh for the promise of dawn,

You dance on the frightening gulf of my dreams
And I fall and my fall lasts an age;
The space at your feet splits wide at the seams,
Wonderful girls!
The fountains of heaven are your stage.

LOVE POETRY

I

With a shout
Nimble love leapt out
So brilliantly acrobatic
That the brain in its attic
Was frightened to own it.

With a croak
All the ravens of blood conceal
Remembrance of other births
Until in the light reversed
The future is broken with kisses.

Utter injustice one worldly ordinance
Love chooses love without changing countenance.

II

Her eyes are towers of light
Beneath the brow of her nudity.

Almost as clearly
Repeated ideas
Cancel deaf words

She effaces each image
Erases love and its restless shadow
She loves – but loves to forget.

III

All-powerful evidence of desire
Grave eyes new-born
Suppressing light
The arc of your breasts tendered
To one who blindly recollects
Your hands your fragile tresses
Locked in your head's unconscious stream
Caresses the smoothness of your skin

While your silent mouth
Proves the impossible.

IV

I told you because of the clouds
I told you because of the tree in the sea
Because of each wave and the birds in the leaves
Because of the clatter of pebbles
Because of familiar hands
The eye that is face or landscape
Sleep which colours the sky
Because of the night mist
The network of roads
Because of an open window a naked brow
I told you because of your thoughts and your words
All kisses all faith survives it.

V

The more this was a kiss
The less hands on eyes
Or halves of light
On the lips' horizon
Swirls of blood
Surrender to silence.

69

VI

You, and you alone – I hear the grass of your laughter
You – your head alone lifts you
From the peak of death's dangers
On the tangled raindrops in the valleys
Beneath the heavy light beneath earth's sky
You cradle my fall.

Birds no longer lend me sufficient shelter
Neither idleness nor yet fatigue
Remembrance of woods and fragile streams
On the morning of sudden whims
On the morning of visible caresses
On that great morning when fate meant nothing more.
The ships of your eyes are lost
In vanishing gossamer
The gulf is unveiled for others to tear apart
Your self-created shadows hold no claim on night.

VII

The earth is blue like an orange
Never an error words do not lie
They ring for you no longer
Kissing is easy enough
For lovers and fools
But on her lips all secrets
And all smiles are wed
And what indulgent dress
Believes in her nakedness.

Wasps blossom green
Dawn adorns the throat
With a necklace of windows
Wings shelter the leaves
You have all the joys of the universe
All the sun on earth
In the wake of your beauty.

70

VIII

My love because you understood my desires
Set your lips like a star in the sky of your words
Your kisses in the living night
And the wake of your arms around me
Like a flame in token of conquest
The world is my dream
Clear and perpetual.

And when you are not there
I dream that I sleep I dream that I dream.

IX

When life looks at itself all is submerged
Raising wreaths of oblivion
Dazed at heart through changes
Inscribed in solar algae
Love and love.

Your hands make day in the grass
Your eyes make love at high noon
Your smiles by size
Your lips by wings
You take the place of caresses
You take the place of awakenings.

X

So calm her skin so grey extinct and calcinated
Lassitude of night in frost-flowers painted
No light remains to her nor any form.

In love with love and knowledge of her beauty
She does not wait for coming spring.

Fatigue of night repose and silence
A living world complete between dead stars
Such faith she has in its duration
Shows so clearly when she loves.

XI

She does not know the art of setting traps
Her eyes are only for her beauty
So simple so simple to delude
It is her eyes that hold her back
It is on me she leans for safe support
It is on herself she casts
The flying net of kisses.

XII

Menacing lie cruel and slippery craft
Mouths in the depths of the wells of the eyes
                in the depth of night
And sudden reasons for nets haphazard cast
Desire to invent impeccable crutches
Delusion of snares between the body
                between the lips
Massive patience shrewd impatience
Everything that weighs upon and reigns
Over freedom of loving
And not loving
Everything you do not know.

XIII

In love with the secret that lies behind your smile
Naked the words of love
Disclose your breasts your neck
Your eyelids and your thighs
Disclose all caresses
So that the kisses in your eyes
Show but you entire.

XIV

Sleep bears your imprint
And the colour of your eyes.

72

XV

She leans over me
Heart searching
To see if I love her
She trusts me but forgets
Beneath the clouds of her eyelids
Her head rests in my hands
Where are we
Together inseparable
Living beings
Living man and living woman
And my mind controls her dreams.

XVI

Lips greedy for colours
And the kisses that paint them
Passion stirs languid waters
A wing holds them in its palm
A laugh inverts them.

XVII

With a single kiss
I make you blaze with the whole of your being.

XVIII

Delusion of flesh shuddering pasture
On banks of blood wrenching at light
Sanguine night has hunted her down
Torn at her throat in the throes of the storm
Forlorn victim of shadows
Of sweetest steps and limpid desires
Her brow no more will be the haven of certain sleep
Nor her eyes the freedom of uttered dreams
Nor her hands the liberators.

73

Quenched of fire quenched of love loving no-one
She imagines pain immeasurable
And all her reasons for suffering disappear.

XIX

Dance of the wind
On a road without end
Leaves fall faster
Clouds hide your shadow.

Lips with the fire
Of ardent ermine
Eyes hunting for light
Kisses the colour of rain.

Night's equilibrium
Snapped by lightning
Thin shafts of fear
Strike at your heart.

XX

I love you at dawn all night is in my veins
All night I watched you
I have so much to learn I am still in the dark
It gives me the strength
To wrap myself round you
To excite your desire to live
In my motionless heart
The power to raise you
To free you to lose you
Invisible flame in the light.

If you should leave me the door reveals the day
If you should leave me the door reveals myself.

74

XXI

Our eyes shut out the light
With light the silence
No more to know it
No more survive its absence.

XXII

Face at the windows like watchers of grief
Sky where I far outstripped the night
Plains so tiny in my open hands
Their double limits dumb inert
Face at the windows like watchers of grief
I look for you beyond all hope
Beyond myself
I know no more how much I love you
Or which of us no more is here.

XXIII

Silent journey
Of my hands to your eyes

And in your hair
Where daughters of willow
With moving lips
Lean backwards to the sun
And four-leaved shadow
Conquers their heart warm with sleep.

XXIV

Habit
Welcomes day as if we hail it blindfold
Love though we hardly think of it
Lies waiting in the brink and on all arms

75

Always
Luck is at her mercy
And empty dreams
So vitally she knows
The reasons why we live.

XXV

I lost you
But love still leads me on
And when I gripped your arms
Pain added to the bitterness
A desert filled with thirst

So I have lost myself.

XXVI

I closed my eyes to see you no more
I closed my eyes to cry
Because I saw you no more.

Where are your hands caressing hands
Where are the eyes day's four desires
You are lost to me no longer there
To dazzle memories of nights

You are lost I see myself live on.

XXVII

Crows beat across the countryside
Night burns out
For a head that wakes again
White hairs the final dream
Hands create day with blood
And caresses

A star called blue
In form terrestrial

Folly of full-blooded cries
Folly of dreams
Folly of sister cyclone's caps
Brief childish folly in the great winds
How was alluring beauty made

You will laugh no more
Ignorance indifference
Do not reveal their secret
You do not know how to make the most of time
Nor how to compare yourself with miracles
You do not listen to me
But your lips share love
And it is through your lips
And behind the mist of our kisses
That we are together.

XXVIII

Red woman in love
To share your pleasure
I paint myself with pain

I lived you close my eyes
Enclose yourself in me
Take then the gift of life

All repetition is incomprehensible
You are born in a mirror
In the image of my past.

XXIX

Absolute essential—a face
Must answer to all names in the world.

CURFEW
(1942)

What do you want the door was guarded
What do you want we were impounded
What do you want the streets were barred
What do you want the town was surrounded
What do you want we were disarmed
What do you want night had fallen
What do you want love is still ours

GABRIEL PÉRI
(1944)

A man died who for his sole defence
Held out his arms to life
A man died who for his only path
Chose that where guns are loathed
A man died continuing the fight
Against indifference and death

And everything he wanted
We wanted equally
Contentment in our hearts
Light shining from our eyes
And justice here on earth
We want them still today

Words there are that make life worth the living
And these are simple words
Like warmth and giving
Justice love and liberty
Words for mild and child
And certain names of fruits and certain names of flowers
Words for courage and discovery

78

Comrade brother both these words are ours
And certain names for village and for country
And certain names for wife and friend
To these we add the name of Péri
Who died so we should stay alive
Remember him whose breast was riddled
His hope lives on we shall not let it end

LIBERTY

On the pages of my note-books
On my desk and on the trees
On the sands and on the snow-drifts
I write your name

On all the pages I have read
On all the thin white pages
Blood and stone and ash and paper
I write your name

On the carved and gilded idols
On the weapons of the soldiers
On the royal crowns of rulers
I write your name

On the jungle and the desert
On the yellow gorse and birds' nests
On the echoes of my childhood
I write your name

On the marvels of the night
On the white bread of the day
On the plighted troth of seasons
I write your name

On all my rags of azure
On the stagnant pond sun-musty
On the lake alive with moon-shine
I write your name

79

On the fields on far horizons
On the feathered wings of birds
On the windmill shadow-circled
I write your name

On each gust of wind at dawning
On the ships and on the ocean
On the madness of the mountain
I write your name

On the clinging mass of clouds
On the sweat of thunderstorms
On the thick insipid rain
I write your name

On all scintillating shapes
On all spires and coloured steeples
On absolute reality
I write your name

On pathways newly trodden
On roadways half-forgotten
On the places springing from them
I write your name

On the glowing lamp ignited
On the blackened lamp benighted
On my houses re-united
I write your name

On a fruit sliced in two portions
Like the mirror in my room
On my bed's abandoned shell
I write your name

On my faithful glutton dog
On his pricked attentive ears
On his clumsy padded paws
I write your name

On the tramplin of my door
On each known familiar thing
On the blessed wave of fire
I write your name

On betrothal of all flesh
On the faces of my friends
On each loving outstretched hand
I write your name

On the window of surprises
On the eager waiting lips
Lips articulate but silent
I write your name

On the ruins of my beacons
On my weak and tumbled shelters
On the rubble of my walls
I write your name

On absence undesirous
On solitude's despair
On stairways of the dead
I write your name

On health at last returned
On dangers past and gone
On hope without regrets
I write your name

And through the power of a word
I can start my life again
I was born to breathe your name
And know you

Liberty

OUR LIFE
(1947)

Our life as you made it is buried
Dawn of a city one lovely May morning
Seized by the earth and enclosed in its grip
Dawn within me seventeen years ever sweeter
Now death enters me as it wills

Our life you said glad to be alive
And give life to all whom you loved
But death has broken the balance of Time
Death came death lived death goes hence
Death visible who eats and drinks at my expense

Death visible Nusch invisible and harder
Than hunger and thirst to my exhausted frame
Pall of snow on earth and under the earth
Source of tears in the night mask of the blind
My past is dissolved and I resign to silence

SPRING
(1951)

On the beach there are pools of water
In the woods are trees mad with birds
Snow melts on the mountains
Apple-boughs glitter with so many flowers
That the pale sun takes fright

Through a winter night in a world ice-hard
I see this springtime close to your innocence
For us there is no more night
Nothing of this that passes can hold you in its grasp
And you do not want to be cold

Our spring is a spring that makes sense

DEATH, LOVE, LIFE

I thought I could shatter the depths of immensity
Through my grief stripped of all contact every echo
I was stretched in my prison with virgin doors
Like a reasoning corpse who had known how to die
A death unlaurelled except by its emptiness
I was stretched on preposterous waves
Solitude seemed more vital than blood

I wanted to tear life apart
I wanted to share death with death
Obliterating all till nothing remained neither window
          nor breath
Nor nothing before nor nothing after nothing made absolute
I had torn the icicle from clasped hands
Eliminated the wintry skeleton
From all desire from life self-nullified

You came the fire then flamed again
The shade gave way the cold below was shot with stars
And earth revived
In your pure flesh and I was light as air
You came and solitude was conquered
I had a guide on earth I knew
Which way to go I knew no limitations
I advanced to vanquish space and time

I went towards you I travelled endlessly towards the light
Life was clothed in hope and raised its veil
Slumber streamed with dreams and night
Looked forward to the promise of the dawn
The sunbeams of your arms half-pierced the fog
Your lips were moistened by the early dews
Dazzled repose replaced fatigue
Love I adored as in my youth

The fields are ploughed the factories bright with day
The wheat is nesting in a swelling tide
Harvest and vintage have unnumbered witnesses
Everything is simple unified

83

The sea is in the eyes of heaven and in the night
The forest gives the trees security
The walls of houses share a common rind
And all roads meet

Men are made to hear each other's voices
To understand to love each other
Have children who in turn will father men
Have children lacking fire and place
Who yet will re-invent new men
And nature and their fatherland
For all men
For all time

Léon-Paul Fargue

(Paris 1876–Paris 1947)

Fargue's great love was for the city where he was born and where he died – Paris, and he was adept at describing its sights and its events. After his early poems (*Poèmes*, 1912; *Pour la musique*, 1914; *Banalité*, 1928) he abandoned poetry for that border-line art, the prose-poem (*D'Après Paris*, 1932; *Lanterne magique*, 1944 etc.). His work had considerable influence on the surrealists.

THE CHILD

Here are my finest
My loveliest verses.
They tremble and flutter
As wounded birds fly.

Can I speak silently
As a flame flickers,
Noiselessly, in the way
That a cock shivers.

Since I seem so shy
And afraid of the simpleton
He is scared in turn,
And wants to give me his hand.

I skip my hopscotch
Like a beautiful bird,
Like the carefree hours
That slink off at a word.
Time with its feverish prattle
Glides softly away . . .

PHASES

The child might very well die
If by running around it gets tired
Of the things it loves.

Where the road intersects we hear
The poor pay their respects
To the silence of broad daylight.

The daily sound, make this your prayer.
Time passes slow and clear
In the somnolent square
Beneath the shivering winter sky.

Life is made for us to suffer,
Blamelessly, without a word,
For nothing at all, or just for pleasure . . .

FOUND AMONG THE FAMILY PAPERS

I've often dreamed, I've often dreamed that I'm
No longer here.
Do not question me, do not pester me,
Do not join me on my Calvary.

Not for me to look for sense or logic,
No right of mine even to think of it,
High time I roused myself and went away.

He has a leave of absence from the dead, he comes.
At the turn of the road that leads to night, I wait.
The sea is reaching for its utmost mark.
A first lamp burns with thirst to light the dark.

A shadow on the pavement. His shadows falls in front
And rests on me, its head upon my heart,
He is there.

Still in a bowler hat, still carrying a brief-case,
Just as he was the day of his return from Italy.
I do not see his eyes. He does not speak to me.

I roll towards him like an obscure stone.
I cannot cross the barrier of his shadow.

How have you been keeping? What have you done since last
We met? Why aren't you riding?
Every day I went to look—you did not come!

No answer did he make to that.
He only said: Remember me.

Then night called him back.

RECALL

He likes to go down to town at the time when the sky closes on
the horizon like a huge moth. He buries himself in the heart of the
street like a labourer in a ditch. The diving-bell of night plunges in
front of windows and shop-windows which spring to light. It appears
that all the glances of evening are filled with tears. The street-lamps
vie with day in an opal of sweetness.

Advertisements scrawl themselves in letters of lava and stretch
across the facades. Rope-dancers stride over the abyss. A great golden
harvester flays a bush full of flowers with its blades. An acrobat climbs
and tumbles in cascades. Castaways wave to strange ships. Houses
advance like the prows of great galleons with all their port-holes
gleaming. The man glides between two bastions of gold like a wreck
towed into port. Cars, dark and streaming, arrive in shoals like sharks
to the plunder of the mighty wreck, blind to the frantic signallings
of men.

Leo Ferré

No anthology of French contemporary poetry would be complete without an example of the work of a 'pop' writer. French popular songs still maintain a character of their own and have not been entirely swamped by American influence. Ferré writes both his own words and music, and, of course, performs his songs.

IF YOU SHOULD GO

If you should go
If you should go one day
You will forget me
Words of love
Do not travel
If you should go away
The tides will soon unravel on the shore
Wild flowers
Will always grow
In laden fields . . .

If you should go
If you should go one day
You will forget me
Wounds of love
Do not bleed
If you should go away
The spring will always feed the hungry sea
New lovers
Still will seek
As fine a day

If you should go
If you should go away
Everything will fade
The things of love
Do not survive
If you should go one day
Death will always pluck the flower of age
This is his work
Despite true love
It cannot stay

If you should go
If you should go one day
Heed what I say
The words of love
Do not fly away
If you should go
And leave the past to turn towards the light
Where prayers
Can reach no more
For ever lost . . .

If you should go
If you should go from me
In these four walls
We'll talk of love again
Just as before . . .

SAINT-GERMAIN-DES-PRÉS

I live in Saint-Germain-des-Prés
And I have a date every day
With Verlaine
The old Pierrot's not changed at all
And when you go courting a girl
Close by the Seine

It's quite likely you'll see
Apollinaire
Coming from slumming down there
With chaps like me
It's crazy
We want to whoop-it-up
No use any more
      We're too hard up.

Look at that crowd of wasters
Penniless poetasters
With dead-white faces
You think it funny
They last a week
But they roll in money
When they squeak
They do pretty well out of dreams
Now it seems
That it's Latin they speak
And they're hungry no more
      In Saint-Germain-des-Prés

You who stroll down the Rue de L'Abbaye
Rue Saint-Benoit Rue Visconti
Close by the Seine
Look at that chap with a grin over there
It's Jean Racine or Valéry
Maybe Verlaine
Now you will understand
You who pass by
How this stony-broke band
Can create such a stink
It's crazy
It makes you think
Salute them
      At Saint-Germain-des-Prés.

SONG FOR HER

Were the four corners of your body formed
Of finest lace I would embroider these
And table-napkins make so full of grace
That we could feed on love upon our knees.

Were your eyes formed from ancient stars,
Those that we still can see but are no more,
I would look beyond the hanging veil
That drapes the frame of heaven with night's azure.

Were your mad tresses swept into a sail
I'ld build a boat and shape it with your heart,
And following the Seine's long winding trail,
I'ld make you Paris—you would be my port.

Should all the long dead suns one day descend
From high celestial plains and fill your corpse
With fire, your modest breasts again would shine
A little with your flame and my desire,

A little with your flame and my desire.

André Frenaud

(Montceau-les-Mines 1907–   )

His poetry and thought have a close affinity to the existentialist philosophy of Jean-Paul Sartre. Often complex both in idea and style, he makes use of regular verse forms, prose-poems, *vers libre* and prose. His earlier poems reflect the mood of the French people under the German occupation. (*Les Rois mages*, 1943; *La Noce noire*, 1946; *Poèmes de dessous le plancher*, 1949; *Les Paysans*, 1951; *Il n'y a pas de paradis*, 1963.)

FRATERNITY

A full net of memories
Why have they hauled it in for me
The eye of my dog the schoolboy
The songs I used to sing for them
The passion for fantasies

I do not know myself in this strange child
I drive away this painful mist
The wind must carry off this tenuous wisp
and leave me all alone in loneliness

But I should like to grasp it as I fly
And reconstruct the man entire until this present age
Him who knew his place and played their games
O warmth which wounds me still today

Pity for you and me since pity is forbidden us
Brothers
to be one sole fraternal entity
before the night's cold breast
united in our mother.

I HAVE NEVER FORGOTTEN YOU

Lacking name now lacking visage
nothing of your eyes no more nor of your pallor

Loosed from the shock of my desire in your elusive image
denuded by the false avowals of time
ransomed by the counterfeits of love
by all these winnings lost
freed from you at last
free as a man long dead
living alone though half alive
toying with stones and foliage

When I slip between the breasts of gentle loves unloved
I still lie clasped in your absence
prone to the living corpse you form
through your power ordained to ruin me
until my final silence.

LOVELESS

a woman speaks

Accept me if the moon is changing
Do not go further from my love
Weevils have bored through the dawn
It is black beyond all belief

No more do the seasons stretch out their ample hands
You have need of a heart at your mercy
I will warm for you once more the colours of the world
If you stay with me—for I am frightened.

TOTAL SOURCE

I want to mount again to the source.
I shall pass the frontier.
I shall go where the great wind rises
before it reveals itself
in looks, in laughs,
in signs which dissipate
the unformed visage.

I am qualified to take you
through still enduring disasters.
I live precariously suspended on the thread
of a voiceless call.
My void is similar to yours.
I shall go on till our two selves
are fused in one.
I shall go on until we return
irrigating, irrigated by the living water.

I knew you as soon as seen
shape of my desire for light.

Beauty blazoned by the absolute,
the triangle, the tresses,
eyes dreamy with sorrow,
the long thigh, the pale skin,
caressed without love,
caressing without love,
indifferent to your gifts or otherwise indifferent,
beauty has created fear from despair,
dazzling, lost, almost dead.

I want to make you give birth,
You who have suffered so much from living,
I want to reconcile you.

All these fires denote wounds.
I want to render them blind,
so that you glitter,
so that I see you.

I shall discover you hidden,
I shall restore you to total life.

The true flame remains invisible
in eyes that carbonize,
but woman has the vocation
of the rainbow and the dew,
of a rainbow painted by desire.

When your face becomes
lovingly purified by happiness
beauty will be achieved.
A beauty attuned to the past
come in advance from the future
in warring deeds innumerable,
changing evil dreams,
perpetually present but evolving
so each is victor in combat.

Already I have captured the flame of your hair,
I have breathed where you inhaled me,
together we stir deep waters.
In the entanglement of our roots
I gather myself, I stretch myself
in the sapwood of our surging blood;
confident in the height of your legs,
arms raised in yours,
I comply where I was forced,
island erupted uncertain,
echo distorted by cold,
irresistible, untenable,
I am endlessly matched in you.

Your openings are all too few.
I need at least another thousand mouths
in our desire for unity.
My perfect love,
I crave the sun for you to drink
until existence vanishes.

We have climbed again from the source
through the triangular fountain
where the basilisk has ceased
to fear its foliage.
We have left nothing to sufferance,
Our delight is crowned with green laurels.
It is the figure-head of chance,
confession of a perpetual choice.
Eyes melted, presence unique.
The depths of the water is clear
and mirrors the inverted sky
where we advance germinating,
a sole burgeon of water,
a sole nest of air in the air.

Eugène Guillevic

(CARNAC 1907–   )

Poet and militant communist, Guillevic's work is highly
individual and seems to owe little to the poets of his
generation. His constant use of short lines and abrupt
statement perhaps reflects the starkness and sturdiness of
his native Brittany, but within these limits Guillevic has
contrived an art which, though muscular, is capable of
the most tender and sensitive expression. (*Terraqué*,
1942; *Exécutoire*, 1947; *Trente et un Sonnets*, 1954;
Carnac, 1961; *Sphère*, 1963.)

IN AMERICA

In America, a great country,
We have brothers.

You will not go
To America

In America, a great country,
There are blacks.

You will not go
To America.

The blacks sing, the blacks fight
In America.

You will not go
To America.

But America is filled with men
Like us.

You will not go
To America.

I want to go to America
To greet them.

You will not go
To America.

I stand for those, I stand for those
Who won't submit.

It's just as well
You will not go.

RECOLLECTION

It is not true that a corpse
Is like a wasted empire
Noisy with vague commands.

That it envies us
When we eat.

It is not true that a corpse
Is blood and milk in a night blacker than ours.

That it's not the dead who laugh in the trees
When the wind howls through the village.

Nor is it the dead
Who make the crockery fall when one's back is turned
Or soot in the fire.

And never a corpse
Who stares with reproach from the eyes of young goats.

There is no need to lie
For there's nothing more dead than a corpse.

But it's true that the dead
On earth maintain a silence
Deeper than sleep.

ANOTHER WAR

While catacombs beneath the torn earth
Still cry out
And flesh still quits the bones of skeletons,

While the children
Of those who go to rot in factories
Have knees as bare
As screws,

While the mutilated sigh
For artificial limbs,

While the Jews
Are still the Jews,
And negroes negroes, their songs
The tears of negroes,

You are preparing for another war.

. . .

You are not hungry
There is little left
For you to envy;
All you need
Is still more power
To endure.

. . .

Disturb the skeleton's repose
To do your will

And see your power
In a world made absolute
Of sand and servitors.

. . .

You know that flowers, everywhere,
Exist for those that work.

You know that space,
The colours of the sky and fields
Are theirs alone.

This you know: it is for these
The frequent day appears.

You know that nothing more
Is yours on earth.

Yet what you want is that
Which trickles through your fingers.

And it's war
You want

Against those who work
Contentedly on earth
To make this world
A festival of toil.

. . .

Bauxite, wolfram, tungsten
For the war.

Planes, lorries, tanks, conscription
For the war.

Convert the factories
For the war.

Enlist the scientists and engineers
For the war.

Foreign buying, national production
For the war.

Hoards of fine materials
For the war.

Supersonic speed
For the war.

Use the stratosphere
For the war.

Operate in polar regions
For the war.

Directed missiles
For the war.

Atomic force
For the war.

Recurrent fever
For the war.

Psittacosis, lead-poisoning, bubonic plague
For the war.

Printing presses, radiodiffusion
For the war.

Women's thighs
For the war.

Basilisks
For the war.

. . .

There's nothing more for you to know
You near the gulf and think you can
Escape, but from this place will grow
For you alone a full-blown rose
While for the rest the hurricane
That blows will sweep them on—
White corpses.

. . .

You stagger.

You are reeling before the gaze of crowds who come
From new-discovered happiness.

The sun is theirs
They have the right to see.

SONG FOR HIS DAUGHTER

My sweet, the sea
You may have guessed
Is not a gift
I can give to you.

My sweet, the wave
Is another world
Where the foot thrusts in
Without repose.

The horizon, my sweet,
Is a noble estate
Which will welcome you
When you open the gate.

My sweet, the briar
You've already seen
Does not make friends
With a fretful child.

My sweet, the dance
I am able to teach
Shines in your glance
And is in your reach.

And hope, my sweet,
Is stronger than the sea
Is stronger than the briar
And the wave and the dance.

BALLADE

All the streams of the earth
Curve towards her dwelling.

All the beasts of the fields
Trudge towards her window.

All the birds of the woods
Rejoice in her beauty.

And the little things
Remember her.

TO THE SLEEPING BEAUTY

You need not
Sleep for ever.

I shall love you.

At no time
Need you fear.

And your body alone
Will shudder with mine.

ELEGY

We had drunk in secret
From flawless glasses
Wine poured out
For us alone.

We had drunk in secret
In the midst of crowds
In search of the sun.

This was on leaving our labyrinths
And our hands were unsure.

A joy for the hill was the sky's azure,
For the summit of trees
And the hovering hawk.

Our moment has passed and we sought
The haven of fields and time everlasting.

We had loved in secret
And we knew that we could not be healed
Of so much joy in so little time.

I HAVE SEEN THE SAND...

I have seen the sand on the shores
And I do not want to die.

I have heard the song of the seals
And I do not want to die.

I have sifted the sand on the shores
And on the sand I have slept.

I have held the sand in my hand
It has drifted away in the wind.

And time was busy with me
Without even knowing or thinking.

I have slept in a cleft of the rocks
By the sand and the ocean.

By its clamour I understand
How the waves break at the foot of the cliff.

I understand the song the seals are singing
And I–I never want
This song to end.

Max Jacob

(QUIMPER 1876–DRANCY 1944)

Poet, novelist, essayist, painter, Max Jacob's first
ambition was painting, and in Paris he was associated
with Picasso and Apollinaire in the launching of
Cubism. Of Jewish birth he later became converted to
Christianity and his poems express the feelings of a
devout mind and a love of simplicity together with a new
interest in folklore and legend. (*Le Cornet à dés*, 1917;
Le Laboratoire central, 1921; *Derniers Poèmes*, 1945.) He
was arrested by the Gestapo in 1944 and died in the
concentration camp at Drancy.

LITTLE POEM

I remember the bedroom of my childhood. The muslin curtains on
the window were scrawled with white lace. I forced myself to discover
the alphabet there, and when I had captured the letters, I transformed
them into designs, imagining H, a sitting man; B, the arch of a bridge
over a stream. But what I liked best were two balls on stone pilasters,
descried through the curtains, which I considered to be the heads of
puppets with whom I was not allowed to play.

IT SO HAPPENED...

It so happened a dream
Intrigued you one night
You looked at an angel
Mere trick of the light.

In her flight Eleanora
Let down her long hair
To hide from Aurora
Her form my desire.

For a faithful husband
No need still to try
I have wings I'm your lover
I teach you to fly.

Let the muse of illusion
At your finger tips bring
Contempt and confusion
For this dream of a shepherd
More proud than a king.

VILLONELLE

Tell me, tell me if you can
What was the song the sirens sang
That made the triremes alter course
And drew the rowers from their oars?

Achilles, conqueror of Troy,
Inside a wooden horse, they say,
Famed Achilles, Grecian chieftain,
By enchanted songs was taken,
Sung by maidens from Hellene.
I implore you, Venus, tell me
What was that lost melody?

At Tripoli a prisoner
Sang a song so fine and handsome
That they did not ask a ransom,
Returned him to his Godmother
Who cried with joy to see him there.

Nausicaa by the pond,
Penelope who spun the wool,
Zeuxis combing locks at home,
All have sung the fol-de-rol! . . .
Songs and songsters all are gone.

Echoed echoes exiles hear,
Echoes heard across the plain,
Where are the songs of yesteryear
They sang again and again?
Where are the girls with charming teeth
Who kept love chained with their refrain?
Let my own songs echo these!

MOON THE COLOUR OF BLOOD

Sadness of waters, Virgin who cowers
Close to a well bordered with flowers!
O huge proliferation!
Prayers that preserve without aid
Of reason my soul from these tears
Of a white-faced child these tears.

Boredom of waiting for news
Coming of winter's drab hues
Ocean, your mattock and spade
Your mattock
A noise in a night of fears.

God sometimes passes us by
In forms that previously
We understood no more
Than all your metaphor
Prophets of doom of the heavens
And here below.

Creaking of wood at the door
A mask! That face I know
It belongs to a lady who died
And left me eternal sorrow.

Sadness of waters we watch ahead . . .
Already my death? Beyond the window
The night the sea and the tide
And those who are dead
The burning bush put out by tempest
And flood
And the moon the colour of blood.

Francis Jammes

(TOURNAY 1868–HASPARREN 1938)

Francis Jammes belongs to no school. His poetry has a touching simplicity and is deeply rooted in French provincial life, its scenes, its joys and sorrows and its piety. (*Le deuil des primevères*, 1901; *Clairières dans le ciel*, 1906; *Ma France poétique*, 1926; *Sources*, 1936; etc.)

PRAYER THAT HE WILL HAVE AN INNOCENT WIFE

Lord, let her that I might have for wife
be humble, sweet, and my most loving friend;
let her when sleeping hold me by the hand;
about her neck, between her breasts, contrive
a charm to dangle on a silver chain;
and let her flesh be golden, smooth and warm
as any plum that sleeps at summer's end;
and let her heart sweet chastity retain
so we can kiss in peace and smile quietly;
let her be strong and keep my soul from harm
as dreaming flowers are guarded by the bee;
and on that day when I must die, allow
but her alone to pray for me and kneel
beside my bed, clasp saintly hands, and feel
in one short gasp the pang of sorrow.

PRAYER FOR A CHILD THAT HE SHALL NOT DIE

Oh God preserve this very tiny child
As you preserve a grass blade in the wind.
Is there nothing you can do, when this mother cries,
To spare his life here for a little while
As though death were not a thing inevitable?
If you let him live, perhaps he will go to fling
Roses next year on Corpus Christi day?
But you are far too good. This is not you my God
Who in the roses on these cheeks implants the blue of death
Unless perhaps you have some lovelier spots for sons
Than in their mothers' arms at the window?
But why not here? Ah, when the hour strikes,
Remember, O my God, faced with this dying child,
You still abide close to your Mother's side.

PRAYER THAT HE WILL GO TO PARADISE WITH THE DONKEYS

When it is time for me to go to you, O God,
let this be on a Saint's day when lanes are dusty
white. And I desire, just as I do down here,
to choose my path to follow as it pleases me
to Paradise, where all day long the stars shine bright and clear.
And I shall take my staff and trudge the highway,
and to the donkeys this is what I'll say: My friends,
I am Francis Jammes and I go to Paradise,
for surely there's no Hell within God's holy lands.
And I shall say: Come, gentle friends, abandon these blue skies,
beloved beasts who with a sudden movement of the ear
brush off the bees, the buffets and the flies . . .

Before your throne, amid these beasts let me appear,
these animals I love so much because their heads bow low
so gently that you pity them, and when they stop, their feet
are placed together daintily, in manner sweet, with toe to toe.
I shall arrive followed by a thousand ears,
by those who carry baskets at their sides,
by those who drag the tinker's wares,
dusters, tin plates, and other things besides;
donkeys of female sex, full as leather bottles,
tottering with double burden; those with little
trousers concealing blue and oozing sores
where clustered flies cling fast and suckle.

Lord, with these poor creatures let me come to you,
let angels lead us peacefully where water swirls
in bubbling streams and cherries bob and tremble
smooth as the flesh of laughing girls.
And, at this resting-place of souls, leaning above
your holy waters, like these donkeys let me be,
who gaze upon their humble and sweet poverty
reflected in the light of your eternal love.

YOU WILL BE NAKED...

You will be naked amid the room's familiar things,
Slender as a reed, as a spindle of light,
And, with legs crossed near to the fire's red wings,
      Will listen to the winter night.

At your feet, I shall take your knees in my arms,
And you will smile, more graceful than a willow branch;
And, placing my head against your soft smooth thigh,
      I shall cry because you are so soft.

115

We shall be proud to look at one another,
And when I kiss your throat you will lower
Your eyes and smile at me, and curve
     Your tender neck to my caress.

Then, when the ailing servant, old and faithful, comes
To knock at the door and tell us: dinner is served,
You will jump up, blushing, and your frail hand
     Will reach for your grey dress.

And while the wind whispers and sighs beneath the door,
While the old clock falters its broken chime,
You will hide your legs and their scented ivory breath
     Inside each slim black sheath.

THE FOURTEENTH ELEGY

My love, you said to me. My love, I replied.
It's snowing, you said to me. It's snowing, I replied.

Once more, you said to me. Once more, I replied.
Like this, you said to me. Like this, was my reply.

Later, you said: I love you. I love you too, said I . . .
The fine summer's over, you said. It's autumn,

I replied. And our words were no longer the same.
Then one day you said: My dearest, how I love you . . .

(This was when the flame of autumn was on the wane.)
And I replied to you: Repeat that . . . again . . .

Pierre Jean Jouve

(ARRAS 1887–   )

Poet, novelist, essayist, Pierre Jean Jouve explores the sub-conscious for his often powerful and disturbing visions; and the sub-conscious in his poetry finds expression in what may be described as spiritual eroticism. The D. H. Lawrence of French poetry. (*Les Noces*, 1928; *Du paradis perdu*, 1929; *Sueur de Sang*, 1934; *La Vierge de Paris*, 1944; *Ténèbres*, 1964.)

SONG OF GRATITUDE

Song of gratitude to the vast World
To its suns and its oceans, its asperities, its abysses
And to the inward heart still more replete with mysteries
With its agonies and its ecstasy
Its dreadful deviations, its eternal strength!
'O sorrow! O grief! Time feeds on life'–
This song of gratitude is also a song of experience
For all those who must feel passion stirring beneath the sky
Must follow must engender by opposing strength to strength,
And not a day to waste, the snows of olden-time no longer melt.
Not a soul so poor who understood nothing
Of that which life desired to say and not a shadow cast
Not explained by a sun.
So the poet, lacking audience, tries to capture
The song of the first lark
Since God did not want the morning to be devoid of love.

MOZART

To You when I listened to your summer rainbow:
Happiness began in the middle regions of the air,
The sword stabs of sorrow
Salved in a thousand effusions of clouds and birds.

A columbine forgotten by the scythe
Delighting day in the meadow,
Nostalgia released such bitter sweetness –
Do you know Salzburg at six in the summer?
Shiver of pleasure, the setting sun swallowed by
     a cloud.

A shiver – at Salzburg in summer.
O joy divine you soon will captive die, O youth imagined!
One day alone surrounds these very hills,
It has rained, finish of the storm. O joy divine
Pacify those people who close their eyes
     in all the concert halls of the world.

SKY

Sky great sky lacking blemish weight or breath
Sign and place of whirlwinds Temple complete and blue
Vast vision severing blind happy nothingness
From what is here in stone and suffering below

Lured from its grief as though by sirens of the sea –
Viewing your infinite inaccessible disdain
Infinite or preposterous and bitter
One single azure target its anxious aim

Sky substance of God! Symbol surpassing aether.

NAKED TRUTH

When will the rapture of hope recapture
This lovely thought this lovely nude
Love unique to the Conqueror of pain
When will humiliated strength return again

When—my poem having created a world
Alone, real, crossing the frontiers of death in one sole act,
Light eternal and blue mountains on the wave—
Shall I be master oblivious to fate

Who gazes on the door of God? and does not tremble.

HELEN SPEAKS

Lead me through this corridor of night
Lover pure lover of darkness
Near to palaces buried in regrets
Beneath forests of flesh of scent of sweetness
Intersected by the marble of the waters
More terrible than any ever seen! And who are you
Unutterable son and pure pleasure
Hiding your flushed member under a cloak
And what do you desire to seize on my once living breast
Within my secret fold burdened with the shadows of death
Why do you come to the opacity of my valley of stones?

HELEN'S COUNTRY

Here lived the incomparable Helen

Here in this ancient place of green and silver
The tears of the cliffs
A blue and pensive sigh broken
By a black up-surge of silvery rocks

Inhuman unimaginable in trailing robes
How beautiful she was clothed in crags
And garbed in flowers of grass! In the long nights
Of tall white mansions bare and barred

How naked and sad she was! and what love was in her hands
And what strength in the dewy splendour of her loins
She had for loving and for living! and her breast
For nursing! and the sweet thoughts
Of her shadow! and well she knew how to die
In a kiss brimming with palm trees and valleys.

Here are her tears
Preserved in this green corridor of the burial ground
A large walnut-tree asleep through the day
Guards tombs the colour of pearls at its feet
And touches the leaning ice of the glacier
Glittering on the opposite bank
Where five silver teeth deformed by sadness
Shine
On the gulf in a harmony of eternal warmth.

Meadow of day! with waves and forests
Of sparse green and sky-hewn rocks
Your celestial purity cries of cruelty
Of evil, as though death itself walked here.

Did Helen love these glaciers and nut-trees
Did her bare arm move across these mountains
Did her dress kiss these fields
Did she seek hope and the light of gold
In the eyes of her young lover?

Far away, Helen's crags
Carved by the sun of funeral obsequies
Gleamed among the hard black peaks
And the sun ripped asunder true religion.

Valery Larbaud

(VICHY 1881–VICHY 1957)

Poet, novelist, essayist, his work is the expression of his cosmopolitan love for cities, for culture and travel. While still young he was stricken with paralysis, but through the mind of his invented character, A. O. Barnabooth, to whom he attributed his poetry (*Les Poésies de A. O. Barnabooth*, 1913) he continued his imaginative voyaging and so enriched the pages of French literature.

THE MASK

I always write with a mask on my face;
Yes, a mask in the old Venetian style,
Long, depressed in front
Like a large white satin snout.
Seated at table and raising my head
I look at myself in the mirror, opposite
And turned three-quarters round, I can see
This childish bestial profile which I love.
Oh, that some reader, my brother, to whom I speak
Through this light and lustrous mask
Would come and place a slow and weighty kiss
Upon this downcast shape and this pale cheek,
And thus impress more firmly on my face
This other face so hollow and perfumed.

MADAME TUSSAUD'S

It seems to me that all the wisdom of the world
Is in the eyes of these good men of wax.
I want to be incarcerated here all night,
A winter's night, quite by chance,
For preferance the Chamber of Horrors,
Home of good wax criminals,
Faces shining, eyes dull, bodies—what?
But are these figures really true?
If so, why have they gaoled, electrocuted, hung them,
While their dumb images remain in here?
With eyes that cannot tell the horrors they've endured,
But who encounter eyes all round them, endless eyes, endless.
At least they're closed at night?

TRAFALGAR SQUARE AT NIGHT

Don't you think, young beggar-girl, that it is lovely,
A most precious thing, simply to be here,
Wandering in this architectural waste
At the centre of the greatest city in the world,
Beneath the perpendicular stars, malignant stars, twinkling
Misty street lamps of the celestial city?
Think no more of hunger, but try
To understand these lions crouched in blue mist,
On the border of terraces of black water where
Livid reflections of electric lights lie stagnant . . .
Come! I am a wizard and I love you, soon
You shall have a banquet laid for you alone
        and flowers in your coach;
Only come and watch a few more moments
This great nocturnal thing, more beautiful

Than deserts, or the sea, or tropic floods
Rolling in moonlit splendour;
Oh, look in silence, clinging close to me,
Woman dedicated to this city!

THE UNNAMEABLE

When I die and go to join our cherished dead
Passer-by, spare one thought for me at least,
You who have jostled me so often in your streets.
Will there remain within my poems images
Of many countries, many glances, and all those faces
Seen so fleetingly in the surging crowd?
I have walked among you, careful of traffic,
And stopped to gaze at shop displays like you,
My eyes have looked admiringly at Women;
I have gone gaily to pleasures and to glory,
Believing in my heart of hearts that this had happened;
I have walked with the herd in delight,
For we belong to the herd, I and my aspirations.
And if, alas, I differ from you all,
It is because I see
Here in your midst a divine apparition,
Before whom I cast myself to be bruised,
Branded, forgotten, exiled,
Ten-fold mysterious,
Invisible Beauty.

Patrice de La Tour de Pin

(PARIS 1911–)

Of part Irish descent, Patrice de La Tour de Pin first
caught the public attention with his *Quête de joie*, 1933,
a collection of poems which spoke with a new voice,
lyrical and classical, expressing the sincerity of a devout
and cultivated mind. In his two more recent volumes he
has gathered his poetic works together in settings of
prose and verse peopled with a mythology of a universe
of his imagination. (*Une Somme de poésie*, 1946; *Le
Second Jeu*, 1959.)

HAMLETS

Rain . . . and then the long wait at the summit,
A brooding sky, washed and inanimate;
A dreary sky, washed to its furthest limit,
The lowest regions of the heart . . .

Climb carefully until the crest is gained,
Reach the hamlets buried deep in shadow:
See how this festive season is proclaimed
And all the lamps of darkness glow.

It comes, a clear reflection from the windows,
The sound of laughter as a child retires
To rest; so close to earth before it goes
To join the magic realm of its desires.

Children, we hear them softly sleeping:
Perhaps on quiet wings borne out of sight;
But now vague shapes are faintly stirring,
The wind itself has vanished in the night . . .

Slow disappearance in the sky's abyss,
A brooding sky, washed and inanimate;
A dreary sky, washed to its furthest limit
The lowest regions of the heart . . .

. . .

We have touched the confines
Of human desperation,
The panacea for pains
We cast out from our door.

But I despise your secrets,
I despise your silence,
Possess you in your absence
Surpassing all before.

ANNIE

When I kiss you while you're sleeping
What befalls my fond caress;
Tell me, Annie, is it lasting,
Does it give you happiness?
In those fields of sweet enchantment,
Lullabies and symphonies,
Do I come as love's pursuivant
Bringing life back with a kiss?

THE ONLY PROBLEM

You sing in order that your heart shall beat
With all the bestial substance of the wind,
The part that suffers, whines and is afraid
And that which urges on the lagging mind.

Then comes a day you know you can contain it
Tight in your mad arms, the final breath
Sensing the rhythm of a heart so like
To yours but far more dumb and near to death.

All the wise men's guile and alchemy,
Science of mind, body intelligent,
Will force you in the end to seek in dying
The secret jewel of such an orient!

THE BULL-RING

If he is a fighting bull
His body full of nobleness
And pride, much better let him live
Than die a shameful death,
Better charge the abject crowd instead
Which goad him on with shouts and yells
And handkerchiefs dyed in white-lead:
Much better they should die themselves.
If he is a fighting bull
He must have blood to spurt and spatter,
If it's mine it does not matter!
Their hearts exude a greasy hate
At what is beautiful and great.

Shame this avid shouting crowd
And feel divinity's proud beat! . . .
—But fools are never touched,
No blood will flow from such,
Only a rancid juice,
Liquor a drowned man spews.
My black bull backward flinching
What can you do in this bull-ring?
A crowd's a contemptible thing,
It can easily smother you.
Will you halt your steps and go?

Split these massed inhumane ranks,
Perhaps reveal and carry off
The one who also jeered and laughed
But burned to feel the noble flanks
Of my great fighting bull.

EPITHALAMIUM

When I come to greet you with all my flesh,
Remoulding the admirable form of woman
With my hands and with my lips, all the light that shines
From your virgin body belongs to me alone,
For no other ocean the river that I am,
For no other sky the cry of joy that I am,
For no other field the seed that I am,
And I seal the body we fashion together,
So, at the last, I can pour my very self into
Your breast and womb, the estuaries of life,
And we can breathe again within each other wind
Sprung from the deepest and most sensual valleys
Beating as one in the rhythm of eternity.

Because you change the whole world with a kiss, let me
Re-animate the great pure forces of your flesh
That, lying dormant, had not found their plenitude,
And through the nuptial moment know that I am merged
In the mighty current binding men's solitude
Since time's beginning, and the divine solitude
That has been theirs, and let us gain this solitude
Ourselves so that the life we make may come to birth.

And let me, beyond my love though still within her,
Remould the admirable form of your own soul,
Illumined with a godlike smile, with the feelings
Of the questing soul about her, as my hands feel
For your body, discovering my natal origin,
And beyond that limitless engenderment of fathers
Reach at last the child who will resemble us . . .

Henri Michaux

(NAMUR 1899–   )

Poet and painter, much of his work is expressed in *vers libre* and prose-poems in which he creates an exotic and nightmarish continent of his imagination. (*Ecuador*, 1929; *Un Barbare en Asie*, 1932; *Épreuves, exorcisms*, 1945; *L'Infini turbulent*, 1957.)

NAUSEA, OR IS DEATH APPROACHING?

Surrender, my soul.
We have fought long enough.
And let my life stop.
Cowards we've not been,
We've done what we could.

Oh! my heart,
You stay or we part,
It's for you to say.
Do not grope in this way at my organs,
Now all attention, now all astray,
You stay or we part.
I can do nothing more.

Lords of Death,
I have neither blasphemed nor applauded you.
Pity me who have travelled so far without baggage or case,
Without master or wealth, while glory took its own course;
You are certainly strong and you're strange – which is worse,
So pity this half-crazed man who cries on your name before crossing
    the bar,

Take him on the wing,
Let him get used, if he can, to your temperaments and your moods,
And if you should deign to help him, give the help I implore.

LABYRINTH

Life is a maze, death is a maze,
A maze without end, says the Master of Ho.

Everything crumbles, nothing is free,
The suicide born to suffer again,

Prison leads to prison,
Corridor follows corridor:

Who thinks to unwind the coil of life
Unravels nothing at all.

Nowhere is anything done,
Centuries live underground
Also,
Says the master of Ho.

Marie Noël

(Auxerre 1883–   )

Her work is notable for its lyric beauty and its profoundly sincere Christianity. (*Les Chansons et les heures*, 1920; *Les Chants de la merci*, *Le Rosaire des joies*, *Chants et psaumes d'automne*, *Chants d'arrière-saison*, 1961.)

EVE

Drink from my flowing breast, my little love,
I am your fountain – Drink! – I am your spring,
Drink this sweet milk which gurgles in your throat
With the soft murmur of a cooing dove.

Lay your cheek upon this tender facet
Of my flesh. Bite me with your little mouth.
I tempt you with the nipple of my breast,
I feel your searching lips . . . Come take it!

Drink, my little greedy, sate your frailty
On me who stoops to pour it out.
Take this warm milk drawn from my inmost self
To reach my bosom's bud . . . Ah! you hurt me!

I know the joy, the sweets of being hurt,
Open and bleeding like a living orange
Melting in honey beneath the toothless gum—
Is nothing left of you when you depart?

Adam! Adam! The joy of being devoured,
Who knows it? Who knows the gentle torture
Of each eager gulp which tugs at me
And draws me to this little changeling coward?

The joy of dying, the sweet adventurous hour,
Blindly lost and lacking eyes and route, moving
In the dark of you who waited for me, tangled
In the promise of your future power!

To die . . . escape from this my solitude,
And from this self which holds my riches captive,
To quench my thirst again, O living water,
And satisfy you with my plenitude . . .

Drink. In your bones I stream—O do not stop!
And when the happy milk glides on its way
A little of myself has vanished in your veins,
A little of myself becomes you, drop by drop.

I listen. Deep in my breast I hear unfurled
The mute and shining clarity of milk.
Adam! do not speak; Adam! I understand
Where went the joy in entering in this world.

LORD WHO HOLDS MY SOUL . . .

Lord who holds my soul in your hand
    Like the wick
Of a blown dandelion which the wind
    Has struck;

Shivering here at the edge of the world,
    Foolish and frail,
Till a puff of your breath speeds it
    Beyond the veil.

What will you do? An immortal soul
    Cannot regain
You, O God, when it flies from your hand
    To a new terrain.

Take care! This is a sorrow too great
      For the wind
To carry still further away
      To waste land.

Preserve my soul in your mouth, O God,
      Like a word
In danger from the searching wind, desire
      Driven mad.

When my immortal seed of anguish
      Flies from death,
Need it go far when you could save it
      With a breath?

Robert Pinget

(GENEVA 1920–   )

Novelist and dramatist, Pinget's novels are a strange and brilliant mixture of the epic and absurd and what is now called black humour. In *Graal Flibuste*, 1956, his fantastic prose is full of poetic feeling and the poem included here is translated from this novel.

THE LOVE QUEST OF
VAOUA THE ENCHANTRESS

Vaoua the enchantress is going hunting, hunting for love,
She has put on her shark-skin shoes and her aquamarine dress,
She has combed her yellow hair, she has put on her crown of pearls,
And to add to it all, she has made her eyes sparkle with octopus blood.
Three thousand dozen oysters she has eaten to titillate desire,
She is there, quivering in the coral reefs, she dives she rises to the
　　　surface.
But she makes up her mind to search for her lovers
　　　down in the deeps where utter darkness makes them
　　　easy to find.
I have seen Vaoua the enchantress desire oozing from all the pores of
　　　her skin,
I was hiding behind a rock and I certainly found her adorable.
But who can claim to love a goddess if she herself
　　　does not want him?
And who can claim to be in love if he is scared
　　　of large amorous women?

You have to be attractive if you want to be loved,
You have to leave your home at night and haunt
    the low-down pubs.
Or better than that, wander amid the sea-weed
    where gloomy shades are restless in the ebb
    and flow of the tide.
Vaoua the enchantress knows all the secrets of the sea
And if I were fish or grain of sand
At once she would find my hiding place.
But I myself am a sea-god too
And when I want to hide I hide, my heart
    belongs to me alone;
This I share with mortal men who are unaware
    of the danger they run
Through keeping secrets neither gods nor men
    will ever know.
Vaoua the enchantress goes hunting for love,
She is off to ravage the small fry, and already
    she rejoices at the thought of stripping
    her victims.
Ah, says she, what a lovely salad we'll make,
I shall bring back a dozen and then we shall see
Who will triumph tomorrow morning, I or they,
    the frail darlings!
My adorable ones, my sweet little fish, my tiny testicles,
Their skin is like peaches, they have raspberry lips,
    bellies of mother-of-pearl and joysticks of sugar,
My sugar-sticks, my creamy sweets.
I play with their apricot bums while they strive inside me.
Now they are all out of breath, wet
    with perspiration
I like their sweat tasting of tears
    and pleasure.
I smooth my tongue between their legs
And feel them harden again and climb
    up beneath me.
My little mountaineers, my honied acrobats,
    my little bumble-bees, when they whisper
    to me in my ear:

'We shall see what we shall see, eh, mighty Trollop?'
Though I let them speak, I could strangle them
But I need their playful tricks.
Our loving done I put them under the douche,
They wriggle like fish—for fish they are—
Then they ask me to rub them, to dab them
    with eau-de-cologne,
And when they are clean, they are fragrant
    and fresh as roses,
Then back into bed and start all over again.
Ah, my mother, venerable Bâth, empress of oceans,
How I thank you for creating me woman,
For giving me these breasts, this belly and this hole so lovely and
    warm
Where the sweet little rods of flesh so busily
    go and come.
At six o'clock in the evening I offer them tea
    and pastries,
They gorge themselves on babas and chocolate éclairs,
The poor little things are quite worn out but their eyes are so lovely,
    so lovely after loving
Though I had made them almost die with delight.
Oh the last one yesterday, how tender he was,
    how sublime.
With his tawny skin and his snow-white teeth!
I was not bored with him, I was past all thinking,
And he laughed and laughed, which excited me more.
We finished by sinking back in the bed and softly licking each other's
    ears
Like two tired animals after a good day's work,

II

But when her money has gone what will
    divine Vaoua do?
At first she'll be old and ugly,
She should really put red on her lips and green
    on her eyelids,

She should really daub herself well with cod liver oil to attract the
    dear little fishes,
But her cunning will be in vain.
You will see her roaming the streets at night,
Shivering in shabby mink, stockings concertinaed, down at heel,
She will end up by telling the tale to earn three ha'pence just for the
    feel of a man's hand.
She will drink all alone in a filthy dive,
But as she's immortal you'll see her
    for hundreds and hundreds of years.
'Vaou, vaou', they'll cry like mythological bitches.
Poor Vaoua, how miserable she will be!
She will sleep in the depths of the sea,
    in far remote places,
Her companions poor old women stinking of urine
    and dirty old men soiling their breeches.
She will squat in a corner all by herself
    close to her pot where mouldy beans rot;
She will nibble a biscuit dropped
    from a liner's latrines;
She will brood on the distant memory
    Of Jack and John, Phillip and Ron,
    Albert and Timothy;
Not even a solitary tear left to shed,
And she'll sleep in her bed belching acidity,
Clutching her stomach.

Jacques Prévert

(Neuilly 1900–   )

First associated with the surrealists in 1930, Prévert soon adapted his talents to the cinema. Immediately after the war he had a great success with his first volume of poems, *Paroles*, 1945; this was followed by *Histoires*, 1946, and *Spectacle*, 1951, which confirmed him as a poet with the unusual gift for achieving popular acclaim without sacrifice of refinement and originality.

THREE LOVE POEMS

I

FOR YOU MY LOVE

I went to the market of birds
    And I bought some birds
        For you
        my love
I went to the market of flowers
    And I bought some flowers
        For you
        my love
I went to the market of scrap-iron
And I bought some chains
        Heavy chains
        For you
        my love
And then I went to the market of slaves
    And I looked for you
    But I could not find you
        my love.

II

SONG OF THE MONTH OF MAY

The ass the king and I
Tomorrow we'll die
The ass from hunger
The king from boredom
And I for love

A finger of chalk
On the slate of days
Traces our names
And the wind in the pines
Calls us by name
Ass King and Man

The Sun's black rag
Wiped out our names
Cold water of Pastures
Sand of Hour-glasses
Rose of red Rose-bush
Roundabout Ways

The ass the king and I
Tomorrow we'll die
The ass from hunger
The king from boredom
And I for love
In the month of May
Life is a cherry
Death is a stone
Love is a tree.

III

The tender and dangerous
face of love
appeared on the eve
of a too long day
Perhaps by an archer
with his bow
perhaps by a harper
with his harp
I do not know
There's nothing I know
All that I know
is that I'm hurt
perhaps by an arrow
perhaps by a song
All that I know
is that I'm hurt
hurt to the heart
struck from above
Burning for ever
wounded by love

BARBARA

Do you remember Barbara
How it rained without cease at Brest that day
And you walked by laughing
Carefree and gay and dripping
With rain
Do you remember Barbara
How it rained without cease at Brest
And I passed you in the *rue de Siam*
You smiled at me
And I smiled too
I did not know you
You did not know me
Do you remember
Remember the day just the same
Do not forget
A man in the doorway
Who called you by name
Barbara
And you ran towards him out of the wet
Dripping carefree and gay
And you flung yourself in his arms
Do you remember that Barbara
Don't be alarmed if I call you pet
I always say pet to those that I love
If only just once it's the same
I always say pet to those in love
Whether I know them or not
Do you remember Barbara
You haven't forgot
That wise happy rain
On your own happy face
On that old happy town
That rain on the sea
On the arsenal
On the Ushant boat

Oh Barbara
War is such stinking rot
What has become of you now
Under this rain of steel
Of blood and steel and fire
And of him who hugged you close in his arms
With so much love
Is he missing or dead or alive
Oh Barbara
It rains without cease at Brest
As it rained before
But it's not quite the same any more
It's a funeral rain dreadful and lonely
Not even a storm any more
Clouds only
Dying like dogs
Dogs that drift away
Downstream at Brest
And float away to decay
Far away so far away from Brest
Where nothing is left.

Raymond Queneau

(LE HAVRE 1903–   )

Poet and novelist, best known in this country for his
novel, *Zazie dans le métro*, 1959, Queneau is one of the
most distinguished and influential figures in the French
literary scene of this century. Originally a member of the
surrealist group he soon found an independent style
and his first novel, *Le Chiendent*, 1933, is a landmark in
the contemporary novel. His poetry is a mixture of wry
humour and extreme sensitivity. Queneau's last volume
of verse, *Le Chien à la mandoline*, 1965, is notable for its
mockery and black humour, and it sounds a new note of
disillusion and despair.

A POEM'S NOT MUCH OF A THING...

A poem's not much of a thing
Scarce more than a cyclone in the Antilles
A typhoon in the China Seas
Or an earthquake in Formosa

Flood the Yang Tse Kiang
And you drown ten thousand Chinese all at a go
Bang
It won't even seem the theme of a poem
Not much of a thing

We've lots to amuse us in our little town
We're about to build a new school
We're about to elect a new mayor and select a new
                market day

149

We were here at the hub of the world now we're near
The ocean mouth that gnaws the horizon

A poem's not much of a thing

CAREFULLY PLACED

Carefully placed and nicely chosen
it takes few words to make a poem
words are all right if one loves 'em
in writing a poem
when a poem is born one isn't alway
sperfectly sure what one's trying to say
so it's vital then to look for a theme
to give it a title
at other times one laughs and cries
when writing with poetic lic-
ence there's always something extreme
about a poem

A CHILD SAID TO ME

A child said to me
I know poems
A child said to me
Poetryseasy

A child said to me
There's lots in my heart
A child said you see
I learn by heart

A child said to me
They know most things
A child said to me
And all by writing

If thpoet could
Fly off on the wind
Children would want
To go with him

OUR NAMES OUR WORDS OUR GRASSES

Our names our words our grasses
desiccate in a vocabulary
licking a calf that has swallowed the prairie
our airs our behemoths our mountains
thick light or heavy but green
while the poster goes grey at the *mairie*
soaking up hatreds of death for ever
and the sun's dial breathes in the gnomon's nostrils
puffing at nature from water-cress heights
where zebras run panting
on winged word and coltsfoot
lassoed by larousse and eternally baptized
to end at the end of a dictionary

FAREWELL

Farewell my earthly round
farewell to my green grass
I'm going underground
I've had my fill of verse
—each poet roundabout
can clatter on in verse
me I've blown the candle out
I'm off to down a glass

IT WAS NEXT DAY

I arrived in the morning it was too late
there was rust all round the kitchen sink
the weight of the stove weighed heavy on the floor
it even warped the tiles it was too late
I should not have known how to put this right even with block and
        tackle objects for which I did not know the words to describe
        them and which I should not know how to use efficiently
mushrooms grew in the earthenware
            washing-up bowl
crockery lay stagnant in the stuffing of the chairs
chairs slept on the hair of the shadows
shadows munched the chewing-gum of the
            dead
I arrived too late it was next day

THE ETERNAL SHORE

High above the goodnights of the eternal shore
the good night of goodbye the night eternally good
high above the blackened vegetation in the shade
of the trees and the grass which sleep and fade
away in the good night of the eternal shores
where a single mollusc clings to the cliff of desire
high above the goodnights of the eternal shore
the man a mollusc clinging to the cliff of desire
scans the coming night and scans the ensuing day
in the vain and fleeting light of the eternal shore
that sees the day no more and sees the night no more

MOULDERING IN THE DUST

When I have mouldered yet a little longer in the dust
What then shall I do no but tell me what then shall I do
No longer will there be the means to step back in the past
Faced by the hollow lie that I shall see myself to be

I knew this right from childhood—and that was not last year—
Even then I wondered whatever I should do
In this sad life so hopeless so bitter dumb and drear
And I knew that one fine day there'ld be nothing left for me

Beside these mournful trees I shall moulder in my bones
And shake the dust from off my feet against the grey milestones
On the road that leads from here to over there—and elsewhere

The little birds all sing within the limits of their frame
And I because they tell me it's good sense shall do the same
But I don't know what to do or even how—to go elsewhere

153

Pierre Reverdy

(NARBONNE 1889–SOLESMES 1960)

Poet and novelist. A poet of great individuality,
Reverdy had a considerable influence on the generation
which followed the surrealists. The best of his poems
are collected in two volumes: *Plupart du temps*, 1945,
and *Main d'œuvre*, 1949.

ON TIPTOE

There's nothing more left
        in my ten fingers
A shadow erased
        at the centre
          Sound of footsteps
Voice that is raised must be smothered
Something groaned but did not die
Something was going too fast
You it was who stopped this magnificent dash
        My pride and hope
            blown away in the wind
Leaves had fallen
        while birds counted
           the drops of rain
Lights extinguished behind the curtain
No need to go so fast
Fear of everything breaking making too much noise

I'M SO REMOTE...

I'm so remote from voices
From rumours of the fête
The mill of froth turns backwards
The fountain's sobbing stops
The hour has slipped by painfully
On the great shores of the moon
And in the confines of this tepid flawless space
I sleep with head on arm
Within the placid desert of this ring of light
Time terrible time inhuman
Hunted on the muddy pavement
Far from the pure circle draining from the glasses
Far from the new-decanted song of idleness
In a bitter medley of grinning laughter
A faded shadow trembles at your roots
Death I prefer obliteration dignity
I'm so remote when reckoning my full account of love

LONG BORNE

Goldfish surprised in the meshes of the wind
Catapults of light
Remnants of thirst tossed to all corners
Triggered release of sated desires
Everything whirled in eddies of captive waves
Your breast booms like hollow ground
There are shadows on the blotting of your cheeks
And crackings of blue china
Over all the purple-tiled roofs
A red intense and denser lacking echo
Vaster blood in the flank of the hill
Migratory birds disorientated

And all those dead men without rhyme or reason
So many desiccated souls
Weightless
Like leaves

MORGUE

Little breast
            O
Clouds
        In the pond where she drowned
        Winter no longer sighs
And
Far from its banks
He passes by having put on his overcoat
Everyone peers at her through the glass
She is dead and smiles at these people
            who do not know what to think
Her little breast seems to move
You are breathing above her
And her eyes close when she sees you
These gentlemen dressed in black
Have eyes that gleam with malice
A little woman I knew well
Misery goes with the wind
And sweeps the avenue
                She had such pretty legs
                She danced she laughed
And now what will become of her
Turning her head
She asks you to leave her sleeping

MR X

He is there
    moving heaven and earth
in his sunday overcoat
And his ways
are just like himself
His monocle monopolises the sunbeams
that slink between us
        He moves towards the church
        But he will not go in
        He says his prayers outside
I think he has waited since childhood in front of the door
    for an angel to come and take his hand and say
Enter you who are my child the other can wait before
    the door
Be not afraid for all things really exist
But behold no-one has ever come
And this morning
The acacias cast their white flowers scenting
    the little square
He dare not kneel by the bench
His prayerbook is useless
Nobody understands what his lips are saying
But I alone have seen his eyes shine and his heart beat
As he came back he seemed to be counting the stones in the street
And he did not see the sunlight stream through the sky
Nor the one who rose without giving him aid.

Saint-John Perse

(POINTE-À-PITRE 1887–   )

Poet and diplomat, Saint-John Perse (the pseudonym of Alexis Saint-Léger Léger) is a great poet by any standards. Couched in verse which owes little to the Claudelian verset or to biblical verse, he has developed a style of high rhythmic originality to express poetry of intense interest and import and a language, sonorous and rhetorical, to match his thought.

Saint-John Perse had a distinguished diplomatic career, in some ways parallel to that of Claudel, but unlike Claudel, on the German occupation he left France to continue the struggle against the invader. For this act the Vichy government declared him a traitor and stripped him of the medals and honours he had won in the diplomatic service of France. Today he lives most of his time in the United States. In 1960 Saint-John Perse was awarded the Nobel prize for literature, and his work continues to be a major influence on the younger poets. (*Éloges*, 1911; *Anabase*, 1924; *Exil*, 1942; *Vents*, 1946; *Amers*, 1960.)

SONG

My horse stopped beneath a tree filled with turtle-doves, I shrill a whistle so clear—no promise that their courses can hold all these out-pourings (Living leaves in the morning are formed in the image of glory) . . .

And it is not as if a man were sad, but rising before break of day and bearing himself with prudence in communion with an old tree, leaning his chin on the last star, he sees in the deep of the hungry sky vast clear events revolving at their will . . .

My horse stopped beneath the tree that cooed, I shrill a whistle clearer still . . . And peace to those about to die who have not seen this day. But from my brother the poet we have news. He has written again a most sweet thing. And some of us have understood.

RAINS

The banyan of rain is established over the
City,
    Polyp weds with polyp raising a sudden reef of coral
in all this milk of living water,
    And Inspiration bare as a retarius combs its mane
of maiden hair in the gardens of the people.

    Sing, poem, your theme the barter
of immense waters,
    Sing, poem, your theme the trample
of escaping waters,
    Full freedom in the wombs of prophetic
Virgins.

    A surge of golden ova in the wild night
of marshes
    And my bed made, O fraud! on the fringes of such a
dream,
    Where the womb conceives swells and blossoms in the
rose obscene of the poem.

    Dread Lord of my laughter, behold earth
steaming in the waste of venison,
    Widowed clay beneath virgin waters, earth washed
of the steps of man's insomnia,
    And, breathed in like uncorked wine, is it
not true it provokes the wreck of memory?

Lord, dread Lord of my laughter! Behold
the reverse of my dream on earth,
   Like the answer of high dunes in the strata
of the seas, behold, behold
   Earth now obsolete, and renewal of time in
languages, and my heart visited by a strange vowel.

II

   Nurses most cautious, Servants with the veiled
eyes of age, O Rains through whom
      the exceptional man retains his caste, what shall we
say tonight, with whom shall we keep our constant vigil?
   On what new bed, from what vexed head
shall we wrest again the worth-while spark?

   Silent Andes above my roof, I sense the clamour
of applause within me, and all for your sake, O Rains!
   I shall plead my cause before you, at the point
of your spears with all the clarity of my being!
   Foam on the lips of the poem like milk
of coral!

   And the dance of my phrases to the spell
of the snake-charmer,
   Inspiration, starker than a sword-blade in the hands
of sentinels,
   Will teach me rhyme and metre to curb
the impatience of the poem.

   Dread Lord of my laughter, preserve me from
assent, from greeting and song.
   Dread Lord of my laughter, for thus it offends
the lips of the downpour!
   For thus it is fraud squandered beneath our
highest migrations!

   In the clear night of noon, we shall proffer
a fresh proposition
   New, on the essence of being . . . O smoke
seen on the stones of the hearth!

And the rain warm on our roof-tops will also
extinguish the lamps in our hands.

III

Warrior sisters of Assur such were the great
Rains marching on earth:
Helmets plumed, tunics looped high, spurred
with silver and crystal,
Like Dido crushing ivory at the gateway to
Carthage,

Like the wife of Cortez, maddened with paint and with
clay, in tall apocryphal plants . . .
They burnished with night the azure on the butts
of our weapons,
They will populate April deep in our chambers'
mirrors!

And never forgetting the sound of their tread on the
sills of the bath-chambers:
Soldiers, O soldiers with spear and dart
sharpened against us!
Dancers, O dancers the ground multiplied
by dance and enticement!

Here are arms by the armful, here are daughters
by cartloads, a granting of eagles to legions,
A raising of spears in the suburbs for
the youngest peoples on earth—shattered phalanx
of dissolute virgins!
O great sheaves unbound! ample and living
harvest reversed in the arms of men!

And the City is glass on its ebony plinth,
science in the jets of fountains,
And the stranger reads on our walls the great
lists of provisions,
And coolness resides in our walls, tonight where
Indian will lodge with inhabitant.

IV

Statements made to the Elder; confessions made
at our doors . . . Kill me, Fortune!
A new language offered from all quarters!
a breath of fresh air for the world.
Like the breath of the spirit, like the
thing itself uttered.

Even its being, its essence, even the fountain,
its birth:
Ha! all the affusions of the health-giving god on our
faces, and such a breeze blowing
In the stream of azuring grass, out-pacing
the progress of distant dissent!

. . . Nurses most cautious, O Sowers of
spores, of seed and airy species,
From what heights dethroned do you
lead us astray,
Like loveliest creatures stoned on the cross
of their wings beneath lowering storms,

What obsessed you so much, that our dream
of living a dream is nearly lost,
Of what other state do you speak so softly
to us that our memory fades?
Did you leave your beds to traffic in holy things
in our midst, O Simoniacs?

At the trade-price of spindrift, there where the sky
ripens its liking for cuckoo-pint and glacier ice,
You haunted the lustful lightning, and deep in forests
of huge torn sap-wood,
To pure parchment striped with a heavenly priming,
You say to us, O Rains! Bring Uncial for this new tongue
and write in letters of green fire.

V

We knew that your coming was full of
grandeur, men of the cities, on our meagre slag-heaps,

But we dreamed of loftier things
at the first breath of the downpour,
  And you restore us, O Rains! in response to our
prayers, with this taste of clay beneath our masks.

  Shall we search for memory in the highest
places? . . . or must we chant oblivion to
bibles of gold in the lowest foliation? . . .
  Our painted fevers in the tulip-tree of a dream,
the mote in the eye of sheets of water, and the stone rolled on
the well's mouth, fine themes to recapture,
beheld

  Like antique roses in the hands of the wounded
in war! . . . The hive is still by the roadside,
childhood in the forks of the old tree, and the ladder
forbidden to lightning's bereaved beauty.

  Sweetness of agave, of aloes . . . dull season
of faultless man! Earth is worn out by the
seared mind.
  The green rains comb themselves at the mirrors of
bankers. Mourners with tepid cloths will blot out
the faces of the daughters-of-gods.
  And Empire builders take into account
new meanings in maps. A whole dumb people
speaks in my phrases, on the wide margins
of the poem.

  Build, build, on the headlands, the catafalques
of the Hapsburgs, the tall pyres of the man of
war, the tall hives of deception.
  Sift, sift, on the headlands, the great graveyards
of the other war, the great graveyards of the
white man on whom childhood was founded.
  And let us expose on his throne, on his throne of
steel, man in the grip of visions which overthrow
peoples.

We shall not end it by watching, trailed across
the sea's extent, the smoke of great deeds when
history burns,
   While in charterhouse and leper-house,
an odour of termites and white raspberries
makes destitute Princes rise from their beds:
   'I had, I had this liking for living among
men, and behold the earth breathes forth an alien
soul . . .'

VI

   Attaining such solitude, a man goes
to the sanctuaries and hangs up his cloak and his
wand of office!
   But I, I carried sponge and vinegar to the wounds
of an old tree burdened with all earth's chains.
   'I had, I had this liking for living far from
men, and behold these Rains . . .'

   Apostates without message, Mummers without
faces, you led me to the bounds of most bountiful
sowings!
   For which of men's fine fiery pastures
did you turn aside your steps one night, for which
tales unfolded
   In flames of roses within the chambers, within the
chambers where lives the sombre flower of sex!

   Did you covet our wives and daughters behind
the bars of their dreams? (In the most secret chambers,
in the care of the eldest, their clear duty conceived like
the feelers of insects . . .)
   Have you nothing better to do with our sons than spy
on that bitter smell virile with the trappings of war?
(like a race of Sphynxes, filled with figures and
enigmas, disputing power at the doors of the
blest . . .)

165

O Rains which cause the wild corn to invade
the City, and stone causeways to bristle with
irrascible cacti,
   Beneath a thousand new steps are a thousand
new-visited stones . . . In trays
fanned by an invisible feather, count your winnings,
diamond merchants!
   And man hard among men, in the centre
of the crowd, is surprised by thought of the sand's lyme-grass . . .
'I had, I had a liking for living the hard way, and
behold these Rains . . .' (Life rises to storms
on the wings of denial.)

   Pass, Mongrels, and leave us to our watch . . .
Such wallowing in divinity when your cloak is of clay.
   All stone washed from tokens of highways, all
print washed from tokens of worship, let us all read you at last,
earth cleansed from the copyist's ink . . .
   Pass, and leave us to our ancient ways.
Let my word again go before me! and again
we shall sing a song of men for him who passes by,
a song of abundance for him who awakes.

VII

   'Innumerable are our ways, and our dwellings uncertain. Thirst
quenched at heaven's fount whose lips are of clay. You, who wash the
dead in the mother-waters of morning—and earth yet with the snares
of war—wash also the faces of the living; wash, O Rains! the sad faces
of the headstrong, the weak faces of the headstrong . . . for their ways
are narrow, and their dwellings uncertain.

   'Wash, O Rains! a place of stone for the strong. They shall sit at
the high table, at the onset of power, those who have not curdled
man's wine, those who have not sullied the taste of tears or of dreams,
the ones who cared nothing for names in trumpets of bone . . . they
shall sit at the high tables, at the onset of power, in a place of stone for
the strong.

'Wash prudence and doubt from the feet of action, wash doubt and prudery from the field of vision. Wash, O Rains! the mote from the eye of the man of good-will, from the right-thinking man; wash the mote from the eye of the man of good taste, from the man of good breeding; the mote from the gifted man; wash the scales from the eye of the Master and from the Maecenas, from the eye of the Just and the Notable . . . from the eye of the man renowned for prudence and decency.

'Wash, wash benevolence from the heart of the Peace-makers, dignity from the brow of the great Educators, and dirt from the mouth of demagogues. Wash, O Rains! the hands of Judge and Provost, the hands of midwives and grave-diggers, the licked hands of the crippled and blind, and the base hands, against men, still dreaming of bridle and whip . . . with consent of the Peace-makers, the great Educators.

'Wash, wash the history of peoples from the tablets of memory: the great annals of office, the great chronicles of the Clergy and academic statutes. Wash edicts and characters and the Claims of the Common man; Covenants, Pacts of Alliance and great federal acts; wash, wash, O Rains! all vellums and parchments, the colour of work-house walls and leper-houses, the colour of fossilized ivory and the old teeth of mules . . . Wash, wash, O Rains! the high tablets of memory.

'O Rains! wash from the heart of man the finest sayings of man: the finest sentences, the finest sequences; the best-turned phrases, the best-born pages. Wash, wash from the hearts of men, their liking for cantilenas, for elegies; their taste for villanelles and rondeaus; their ample felicity of expression; wash away the attic salt and the honey of euphemism, wash, wash the clutter of thought and the dregs of knowledge: from man's heart with no denial, from man's heart with no loathing, wash, wash O Rains! the finest gifts of man . . . from the hearts of men gifted for great works of reason.'

VIII

The banyan of rain loosens its grip on
the City. It drifts away on the winds of heaven
    As it drifted among us! . . . And no use
denying that, suddenly, all came to nothing.

167

Who wants to know what it happened through rains
in progress over the earth, that it came to live on my roof,
amid signs and portents.

Promises broken! Sowings untiring!
And smoke beheld on the highways of men!
     Came the lightning, ha! now it quits! . . . And
we shall lead you back to the City gates
     Great Rains in progress through April, great
Rains in progress driven by the whip like an
Order of Flagellants.

But behold us naked and more exposed to this reek
of humus and benzoin where earth awakes to the taste
of virgin black.
     It is earth refreshed in the heart of the
fern-brakes, the outcrop of fossils in streaming
marl,
     And in the sorry pulp of roses after the storm,
earth, earth has again the likeness of woman made woman.

     . . . The City has sprung to life in the blaze of a thousand
swords, the flight of falcons in marble, the sky
again in the basins of fountains,
     And the golden sow at the stele's base in deserted
places. It is splendour again at cinnabar
porches; the black beast shod with silver at the lowest
door of the gardens;
     It is desire again in the wombs of young widows,
young widows of warriors, like great
urns resealed.

     . . . It is fresh air flowing on crests of
anguage, foam again on the lips of the poem,
     And man again everywhere urgent with
new ideas, which yield to the restless surge
of the spirit:
     'The song, the wonderful song beheld in the
ebb of the waters! . . .' and my poem. O Rains!
which was not written!

IX

Night has come, the barred gates close, what is the weight
of heaven's water in the depths of the dark ages?
     At the glittering point of the spears of my
being! . . . And all being equal, in the scourge of my spirit,
     Dread Lord of my laughter, tonight you will carry the
slander on high.

     . . . For such are your delights, Lord, at the
bleak dawn of the poem, where my laughter appals
the green peacocks of glory.

Nathalie Sarraute

(IVANOVO, RUSSIA 1902–   )

Novelist and essayist, and one of the principal figures in
the development of the 'new novel'. Her *Tropismes*,
1938, was her first attempt to break loose from the
shackles of the conventional novel, and consists of a
series of brief and elusive word pictures which explore,
in a completely new way, the borderland of the sub-
conscious. The dividing line between Sarraute's prose
and the prose-poem is so tenuous that a place has been
found for examples in this anthology of the work of
a highly original and poetically gifted woman. (*Portrait
d'un inconnu*, 1944; *Martereau*, 1953; *Le Planétarium*,
1959; *Les Fruits d'or*, 1962; *Entre la vie et la mort*, 1968.)

TROPISM 14

Although they were silent and kept themselves to themselves,
modestly bent, quietly counting a new row, two stitches to the right
now three under and now a row above, so feminine, so efficient
(don't pay attention, I'm all right like this, I ask nothing for myself)
they felt increasingly, as if by a prickle in their flesh, her presence.

Still staring at her, as though fascinated, they watched terrified for
each word, the faintest inflexion, the subtlest nuance, each gesture,
each look; they went on tiptoe, turning round at the slightest sound,
for they knew that everywhere there were mysterious places they must
not bump against, must not brush against, or else, at the slightest
contact, little bells, as in a tale of Hoffman, thousands of little bells
with clear notes like her virginal voice – would start to tinkle.

171

But sometimes in spite of all precautions, of all efforts, when they saw her standing under the lamp, looking like a soft and fragile under-sea plant decked all over with wavering tentacles, they felt themselves slide, falling with all their crushing weight beneath them: that produced stupid jokes, sneers, frightful tales of cannibals, blurted out unable to restrain themselves. And she softly backed away—oh! it was too frightful!—thought of her little room, the dear refuge where she would soon kneel down when she went to bed, in her linen nightdress gathered about the neck, so childlike, so pure, a little Thérèse de Lisieux, Saint Catherine, Blandine . . . and gripping in her hand the little gold neck-chain, prayed for their sins.

Sometimes too, when all went well, when she had curled herself up already, feeling on the verge of one of those questions which she loved so much, when one discussed them sincerely, seriously, they made off with the twirl of clowns, faces stretched in idiot grins, horrible.

TROPISM 17

When it looked as though it would be fine, on holidays, they went for a walk in the suburban woods.

The brushwood thickets were pierced by crossings on which narrow avenues symmetrically converged. The grass was sparse and trodden, but on the branches new leaves had started to bud; these did not succeed in casting around them any of their lustre and resembled those children with sour smiles who puckered their faces in the sun in hospital wards.

They sat down to eat at the side of the pathways or in the bare clearings. They seemed oblivious to everything, they were above all that, the cheeping of birds, the furtive buds, the coarse grass; the close atmosphere in which they had always lived surrounded them here too, emanating from them in a heavy acrid steam.

They had brought with them their spare-time companion, their little solitary child.

When the child saw that they had started to settle down in the spot they had chosen, he opened his folding stool, placed himself by their side, and crouching, began to scrape the ground, to collect dry leaves and small stones into little piles.

Their words, mixed with the disturbing scents of that scant spring, full of shadows stirring with confused shapes, enveloped them.

The dense air shiny with damp dust and sap, stuck to him, clung to his skin.

He refused to go far from them to play with the other children on the grass. He stayed there, glued to the spot, and with gloomy avidity absorbed all that they said.

TROPISM 24

They rarely showed themselves, they sat crouching in their apartments, at the back of their dismal rooms, and watched.

They telephoned to each other, prying, remembering, grasping at the slightest indication, the faintest sign.

Certain of them delighted in cutting out the advertisement from the paper disclosing that her mother required a daily dressmaker.

They thought of everything, they watched jealously, holding hands in a close packed circle, surrounding her.

The lowly sisterhood, faces half obliterated and dulled, maintained their circle around her.

And when they saw her grovelling shamefully and trying to slip between them, they quickly lowered their interlocked hands, and, all huddling together about her, stared at her with vacant and obstinate looks and wilfully infantile smiles.

Jules Supervielle

(MONTEVIDEO 1884–PARIS 1960)

Poet, novelist, dramatist; born in Uruguay of Basque origin, much of Supervielle's poetry is rooted in the country of his birth, but there is also a metaphysical lyricism which gives his poems their own individual and distinguished quality. (*Débarcadères*, 1922; *Amis inconnus*, 1934; *La Fable du monde*, 1938; *A la Nuit*, 1947; *L'Escalier*, 1958.)

WHAT DO I CARE...

What do I care for the fragrant ring of mountains,
    The stabbing sun on the plains,
    The rock's sister the goat,
And, lord of the landscape, the stubborn oak.

No more do I know you, Nature, nor hear your cries,
    Nor heed the martyred horizon,
I am here amid tree and reed
Like the river—without reason, without eyes.

THE WAY AHEAD

Do not touch the shoulder
Of the rider passing by,
For he will come again
At nightfall then,
A starless night with neither
Cloud nor crescent moon.
—What will become
Of all that forms the sky,
The moon's slow circle,
And the rumour of the sun?
—You must stay
Until a second rider
As mighty as the last
Consents to pass.

MATHEMATICS

Forty children in a room,
A blackboard and a triangle,
A circle hesitant and dumb
Its centre beating like a drum.

Letters lacking words and country
Stare in blank expectancy.

Escarpment of a trapezoid,
Voice sing-songing in the void,
And the problem with a snarl
Wriggles round and bites its tail.

Jaw of angle, gaping gulf,
Is it bitch or is it she-wolf?

Figures every shape and size,
Busy ants that first dismantle
Then re-build their teeming ant-hill
Glazing dazing children's eyes.

THE PORTRAIT

Mother, I am lost when I try to find the dead,
Lost in my soul, its precipitous cliffs
And tangled ways.
Help me return
From horizons which drain vertiginous lips,
Help me to rest,
So many actions part us, such cruel hounds!
When I lean above the fountain formed by your silence
Your soul, in a shiver of leaves confounds the reflections.
Ah! in your photograph
I see no breathing likeness,
Yet we must go together, your picture and I,
Condemned to one another;
Hand in hand we walk
In this clandestine land
Where nothing moves except ourselves.
Strangely we scale the heights of the mountains
And linger descending as if our hands were hurt.
A candle gutters night by night, and splutters in the dawn,
A dawn which day by day discards the heavy shroud of night,
Half smothered,
And hardly knows itself.

Harshly I speak to you, my mother;
Harsh I am to the dead because I must
            be harsh,
Balanced upon these shifting roofs
Hands cupped to mouth in a megaphone, shouting in rage

To master this all deafening silence
Which separates the living from the dead.

Some of your jewels I have — ice-floes of winter
Drifting down broad rivers;
This bracelet too was yours now burning in its case
On this oppressive night when the crescent moon
Tries in vain to rise
And tries again, chained to the impossible.

My strength resides in you, I who am so weak
We are so linked together that together we should die,
Drowning like ship-wrecked sailors, flailing their feet,
Striving to keep afloat in the drear Atlantic deep
Where fishes are blind
And horizons steep.

Because you have been me
I can gaze at a garden thinking
            of nothing else,
I can choose where to look,
Go out and meet myself.
Perhaps there still remains
One finger-nail from your dear hands among my finger-nails,
One single eyelash fast enmeshed in mine,
One of your heart-beats strayed among the heart-beats
            of my heart,
This bond we have in common
And this bond I shall retain.

Does my heart still beat? You have no further need
            of yours,
You live a life apart, sequestered, as though you were
            your sister;
Eight and twenty years of death
Are watching me, three-quarter length,
Poised and self-possessed.
The dress you wear is still the same and never
            will wear out,
It entered in eternity so softly,

Sometimes the colour changes but I alone
          know this.

Copper cicadas, lions of bronze, vipers of clay,
Here nothing breathes!
Only the breath of my illusion
Haunts this place.
But on my wrist
The mineral pulse-beat of the dead
Is heard as I draw near the corpse
That in the tiered grave-yard lies.

Paul Valéry

(Sète 1871–Paris 1945)

Poet, essayist, dramatist, philosopher; a poet whose work was a turning-point in contemporary French poetry and whose meticulous mind was devoted to a life-long search for perfection. After his early work, *Album de vers anciens*, 1890-1900, he published no more poetry until *La Jeune Parque*, 1917. *Charmes*, 1922 contains his masterpiece, the great elegy on death, *Le Cimetière marin.*

THE CEMETERY BY THE SEA

My soul, do not seek the life of the immortals but enjoy to the full that which is within your reach.
PINDAR (Pythic Ode III)

This quiet roof where walk the doves
Quivers between the pines, between the tombs;
High noon in living fire enfolds the sea –
The endless ever moving sea –
O what reward, what recompense for thought,
To gaze upon the god's tranquillity!

What pure intent in minute diamond flashes
Is squandered in an imperceptible foam;
What peace is here engendered
When poised above the abyss rides a sun –
Clear evidence of one eternal cause –
Time glitters and knowledge is the Dream!

Strong treasure house, stark temple to Minerva,
Calm mass and visibly aloof,
Solemn Water, great Eye who stores within
So much of sleep beneath a veil of flame,
O my silence! . . . Edifice in the soul
Crowned in the gold of a thousand tiles, Roof!

Temple of Time achieved in one sole sigh,
To this unsullied spot I climb, attain
A sea-girt, sea-embracing vision, while,
In sacrifice supreme unto the gods,
The shimmering light serenely strews
About the height a sovereign disdain.

Like to a fruit which joyfully dissolves
Within the mouth and in delight
Resolves and dies, here I inhale
The smoke-drift of my future life,
And the sky, to the incinerated soul,
Sings the mutations of the murmuring shores.

Fair sky, true sky, look on one who changes
After such pride so strangely indolent,
Filled now with a new and potent strength
Launched in this radiant space, self-immolated,
Above the houses of the dead my shadow moves
And tries its frail wings.

Pitiless, the solstice burns my shieldless soul;
Just law of light, I brave your brands,
I face your armoured might
And yield to you your rightful place!
Look on yourself! . . . though thus to yield
Implies a mournful half of shade.

For me alone, to me alone, in me alone,
Close to the very core, the poem's fount,
Between the void, between the pure event
I wait the echo of my greatest self—
A sound eternal, bitter, dark and sombre
Sounding the hollow depths of dim futurity.

Do you know, false captive of the leaves,
Gulf-eater of these meagre lattice bars
Blinding the secrets of my dazzled eyes,
What body drags me to its futile end,
What head attracts it to this charnel ground?
One single spark thinks of my absent dead.

Holy enclosure, filled with immaterial fire,
Terrestial fragment tendered to the light,
This place pleases me . . . By torches dominated,
Of gold, of stone, of solemn pines created
Where marble trembles in a shadowed pall,
The faithful sea sleeps there upon my tombs.

Superb Hound! Keep the idolator away!
While solitary, heedless of time, I smile
As I shepherd these mysterious sheep,
The white flock of my quiet graves,
Keep far afield the prudent doves,
Vain dreams and prying angels.

Once here the future is but idleness,
The insect grates and scrapes the arid ground,
All is burnt, decayed, melted in air
And thinned to an essence inconceivable;
Life is vast, drunk deep with absence,
And bitterness is sweet, the mind is clear.

The hidden dead are happy in this earth,
It warms and dries their mystery.
Noon high above, noon motionless,
Conceived in self, sufficient in itself . . .
Head complete and perfect diadem,
I am the secret change within,

You have but me alone to curb your fears!
My griefs, my doubts and my desires, these
In your great diamond are the flaw . . .
But in the night a people vague,
Weighed down by marble, shrouded in the trees,
Have suffered there your slow remorseless law,

And foundered to thick nothingness,
White species swallowed by red clay,
The gift of life has passed into the flowers.
Where are the common phrases of the dead,
The personal art, the minds unique?
The worm crawls where eyes once filled with tears.

Shrill cries of girls in amorous excitement,
The glistening teeth, the brimming eyelids,
Delicious breasts that play with fire,
Sanguine lips aflame with fierce desire,
The final gifts, the fingers that defend them,
All goes beneath the earth, the game begins again.

And you great soul, is it a dream you hope for,
A dream no more the web of coloured lies
Which fleshly eyes weave of waves and gold?
When you are vapour, tell me, will you sing?
Come! All vanishes! My presence here is porous;
Holy impatience also dies.

Brief immortality in black and gold,
Cold comforter in laurels fearfully decked
That makes of death a mother's breast,
Fine lie and pious ruse!
Who does not know and who does not refuse
That empty skull and that eternal grin.

Fathers profound, heads uninhabited,
Who beneath this weight of shovelled earth
Are earth itself infirm to human tread,
The true, the gnawing irrefutable worm
Is not for you who sleep beneath the slab,
He lives on life, me he will never quit.

Love, perhaps, or hatred of myself?
His secret tooth is ever at my heels,
All names are his, no name that does not suit!
Useless! He sees, he needs, he dreams, he feels!
My flesh delights him, no escape in sleep,
I live as liege to this all-living thing.

Zeno! Cruel Zeno! Zeno of Elea!
Have you transfixed me with that arrow on the wing
Which quivers, flies, yet does not fly?
Its twang is birth to me, its barb death's sting!
Ah! the sun . . . Tortoise shadow on the mind
That halts Achilles in his stride.

No, no! . . . Stand up and face the coming tide!
My body, shatter this brooding shape!
My breast, drink deep the new-born wind!
The chill sea-air, the salt sea-breath —
O mighty sea! — restore my soul;
Run to the wave and spring from it afresh!

Yes! Huge sea inspired with bacchic frenzy,
Your panther skin and chlamys pierced
With a myriad idols of the sun,
Absolute Hydra, drunk on your own blue flesh,
Gnashing your flashing tail
In an uproar loud as silence,

The wind is rising! . . . I must try to live!
The vast air tosses the leaves of my book,
The wave leaps high in powder on the rock.
Scatter in flight, white bedazzled pages!
Break waves! Break with rejoicing waters
This quiet roof where pecked the sailing doves.

Epilogue

to be recited

                at the

                                burial of poets

Saint-Pol Roux

(SAINT-HENRY, BOUCHES-DU-RHÔNE 1881–BREST 1940)

> Poet and dramatist, Saint-Pol Roux's poetry is both magnificent in style and complex in texture (*Les Reposoirs de la procession,* 1893; *Anciennetés,* 1903). At the end of the last century he was associated in Paris with the symbolists, but he soon retired to his native Brittany where he spent the rest of his long life. Interest in his work revived when in 1925 the surrealists claimed him as the forerunner of surrealism. He died a martyr's death while trying to protect his home from the German invader.

TO BE RECITED AT THE BURIAL OF POETS

Tread gently, Grave-diggers.

Tread very gently, for this coffin is not like others which hide mere clods of clay swathed in shrouds, this one conceals a treasure within its planks covered by two very white wings as if unfolding from the fragile shoulders of angels.

Tread gently, Grave-diggers.

Tread very gently, for this chest is filled with a harmony contrived of an infinite variety of things: cicadas, scents, garlands, bees, nests, grapes, hearts, ears of corn, fruit, thorns, claws, talons, moans, chimeras, sphinxes, dice, mirrors, cups, rings, amphorae, quivers, thyrsis, chords, cap-and-bells, peacock, carillon, diadem, rudder, crozier, yoke, joker, rod, sword-blade, chains, arrow, cross, necklace, serpents, mourning, lightning, bucklers, trumpet, trophies, urn, clogs, buskins, breezes, waves, rainbow, laurels, palms, dew, smiles, tears, sunbeams, kisses, gold . . . all this in one gesture too swift to vanish or dissolve.

Tread gently, Grave-diggers.

Tread very gently, for though the stature of man is small, this silent marble contains a crowd without number and gathers more characters and effigies at its centre than a circus, a temple, a palace or a forum; do not jostle therefore these various symbols and thus disturb the peace of a universe.

Tread gently, Grave-diggers.

Tread very gently, for this apostle of light was Beauty's chevalier, she whom he served most courteously despite the sarcasms of some and the spittle of others, and, in this mystery, you will make the foremost of womankind sob if you lay her lover too roughly in the ground.

Tread gently, Grave-diggers.

Tread very gently, for perhaps he was a god, this poet, a god we elbowed without suspecting his sceptre, a god who offered us pearls and hyssop from heaven while we flung malice at him and husks from his table, a god whose going surely casts us into terrible darkness; and that is why your tools of sleep conjure a sunset at this very moment.

Tread gently, Grave-diggers.

But what you are doing there is it not only a semblance? We have followed heaped roses on the hypothesis that it was a body and that in this trench into which you are about to descend, O treasuries of ashes, and these obsequies therefore will be but an ample apotheosis and we shall discover ourselves faced by a miracle. Oh, say this hero has not ceased to live, grave-diggers, this hero is not dead since his soul still vibrates in his books and will enchant the world's heart for long in spite of centuries and tombs!

Tread very gently, Grave-diggers.

Humbly he wanted to submit himself to the common law of human beings, breathe his last sigh and die like us, who follow after, proud that this man had the brow of a god, resurrected before the kneeling multitudes. Truly, I say to you, he goes to his dwelling-place to be born our Master once more from among these dead guarded by cypress and sycamore, and know that on leaving this enclosure of Time, we shall find him still standing in our memories, so tomorrow, on the scattered plinths erected to glory, we shall find him sculptured in the sturdy piety of all humanity.